D0425620

Are We There Yet? is a must read for every married couple and every person contemplating marriage. This book is a wonderful journey into what makes marriage the blessed relationship God intends it to be. The transparency of Dr. and Mrs. Chappell along with the clear teaching of biblical principles will not only help every couple make their marriage *work;* it will allow them to make their marriage *great.*

DR. AND MRS. MICHAEL EDWARDS, Pastor, Heritage Baptist Church, Woodbridge, Virginia

Okay. You may think you have read it all on the subject of Christian marriage, but we believe that you will, like us, find yourself enjoying this literary journey immensely while at the same time being edified biblically for the husband and wife pilgrimage. We didn't want to put this book down! Weaving their personal travel experiences (including pictures) into a narrative format to teach relevant scriptural truth on how to have a great marriage is brilliant and immensely captivating. Everyone needs to read this masterpiece.

DR. AND MRS. PAUL KINGSBURY, Pastor, North Love Baptist Church, Rockford, Illinois

In a culture that is constantly attacking faithful Christian marriages, there is a great need for biblical marital counsel. Dr. and Mrs. Chappell do a tremendous job of presenting biblical principles and personal illustrations that will be a help to every marriage. We were encouraged and helped by this book, and we look forward to sharing it with others on their marriage journey.

DR. AND MRS. MIKE NORRIS, Pastor, Franklin Road Baptist Church, Murfreesboro, Tennessee

Our dear friends, the Chappells, have written a wonderful book on marriage. It is refreshingly candid, scripturally robust, and engagingly practical. Any couple, from engaged to newlyweds to seasoned spouses, will be helped by this excellent resource.

DR. AND MRS. R.B. OUELLETTE, Pastor, First Baptist Church, Bridgeport, Michigan

From the beginning to end, these pages are filled with spiritual challenge and practical advice for every couple. Read this book together, and discover principles and purpose for your marriage journey.

DR. AND MRS. TIM RABON, Pastor, Beacon Baptist Church, Raleigh, North Carolina

We do not know of a better couple to write this book than Dr. and Mrs. Chappell. We admire their love and respect for one another and have been blessed by watching their marriage. Regardless of what stage of marriage you are in, this book will help, encourage, challenge, and strengthen your relationship.

DR. AND MRS. DON SISK, Baptist International Missions, Chattanooga, Tennessee

In their very helpful book, the Chappells approach the subject of marriage with a winsome and engaging manner. Their ability to relate to couples in an appropriately transparent way is effective in addressing the most difficult and delicate subjects. We appreciated the comprehensive, direct, and yet simple treatment of the challenges of marriage. With the engaging style and real life stories of Dr. Paul and Terrie Chappell, this book is a great read for happily married couples too! We are happy to recommend this new book both for those just starting out on the journey and for those well along the marriage path.

DR. AND MRS. WAYNE VAN GELDEREN, Pastor, Falls Baptist Church, Menomonee Falls, Wisconsin

ARE WE THERE YET?

MARRIAGE
*A Perfect Journey
for Imperfect
Couples*

PAUL & TERRIE CHAPPELL

First published in 2017 by Striving Together Publications, a ministry of Lancaster Baptist Church, Lancaster, CA 93535. Striving Together Publications is committed to providing tried, trusted, and proven books that will further equip local churches to carry out the Great Commission. Your comments and suggestions are valued.

Striving Together Publications
4020 E. Lancaster Blvd.
Lancaster, CA 93535
800.201.7748

Cover design by Andrew Jones
Layout by Craig Parker
Writing assistance by Monica Bass

The author and publication team have given every effort to give proper credit to quotes and thoughts that are not original with the author. It is not our intent to claim originality with any quote or thought that could not readily be tied to an original source.

ISBN 978-1-59894-353-5
Printed in the United States of America

DEDICATION

To Don and Virginia Sisk
Thank you for modeling a journey of Christlike marriage
for over sixty-five years as together you have taken the
gospel of Christ into regions around the world.
Thank you for being our dear friends and mentors. Some
of our favorite memories of serving the Lord have been
with you along the journey.

CONTENTS

ACKNOWLEDGMENTS

The best travel trips we have been on have always involved significant amounts of preparation and the help of many people. From coordinating times of preaching and ministry, researching points of interest, planning, and packing, there are always more details than the moment of decision to make the trip.

Writing a book is no different. This manuscript is the fruit of many people's investments, and for their labor we are grateful.

Over the years, we have been blessed with role models and mentors whose strong, Christ-centered marriages have blessed and challenged us. The Lord has allowed us to know couples, such as Lee and Caroline Roberson, Don and Virginia Sisk, R.B. and Krisy Ouellette, and many couples in our own local church whose faithfulness to one another over many decades of marriage have been encouraging and helpful.

We also would like to thank the deacons of Lancaster Baptist Church for your love for our family and your encouragement to us over the years to invest in family time. A few of the trips referenced in this book have been your gift to us—thank you. Additionally, we are thankful for your prayers and encouragement as we have invested in times of ministry to missionaries and fellow Christian servants, as is represented in many of the stories in these pages.

An entire team effort is involved in a book such as this. We'd like to thank our dear friends in ministry who have taken the time to review this manuscript and provided helpful feedback: Troy and Teri Dorrell, Mike and Nancy Edwards, Ron and Shelly Hamilton, Paul and Dianne Kingsbury, Jim and Caroline Newheiser, Mike and Mila Norris, R.B. and Krisy Ouellette, Tim and Sharon Rabon, Don and Virginia Sisk, Wayne and Beverly Van Gelderen, and Scott and Jodie Wendal. Thank you to Monica Bass for your writing and editing assistance and to the Striving Together Publications team for embracing our vision for this project and for helping us bring this manuscript to completion.

PREFACE

A NOTE ON TRAVEL AND JOINT AUTHORSHIP

A side from time with our children and grandchildren and serving the Lord and our church family together, one of our favorite things to do together is travel. We enjoy driving through California, seeing what God is doing on foreign mission fields, visiting other cultures, learning history, and just spending relaxed time together.

To be sure, we travel a little differently. I (Paul) have a tendency to push to a destination and not always enjoy the journey. The Bible, on the other hand, teaches us to walk in Christ's *steps*, not to frantically conquer destinations. Our Heavenly Father is interested in every step of the journey, and we believe that, for a married couple, His desire is that we enjoy companionship along the way.

My first experience of travel began when my parents became missionaries to Korea. I learned to enjoy different cultures and foods in Asia and made many friends along the way. Since then, God has blessed me with the opportunity to travel across America and to many far-reaching places to preach His Word. Additionally, Terrie and I have been blessed to travel for purposes of education and family time together. When you live in a community where you are known, we've found it's nice to get away as a family, to relax, grow, and enjoy a new place that God has created. And along these journeys we have enjoyed great conversations, prayer times, witnessing, and fellowship. We've also had our share of mishaps, cancelled flights, and delays. But through each of them we have found a silver lining and a way to compensate for lost time.

The best part of travel for both of us is simply being together. Thus, as we prepared to write this book, we decided to make it travel themed. After all, if marriage is anything, it is a journey.

Although both of us have written in the past, this is our first book to co-author. All of the material in these pages represent both of us. We have spent hours brainstorming together (actually, while on two road trips) and have both pored over every page and made additions and edits to each others' notes. But for ease of expression, we determined to write primarily in Paul's voice. Where it made a difference in understanding, we have noted Terrie's voice throughout.

We pray these pages will be a travel aid to you as you continue the best journey we have ever undertaken together—marriage itself.

Paul and Terrie Chappell
Lancaster, California
May 2017

(left) Leaving Prague

(below) The Cotswolds is a beautiful area of England that borders Wales and is near where the Bible translator William Tyndale grew up.

ONE
DREAM DESTINATION
Direction

I f you really want to get to know someone, you should go on an extended trip together. Between the protracted time together and its unique frustrations, travel has a way of drawing someone's hidden personality to the surface and giving insight into their idiosyncrasies, preferences, and character.

In fact, there are very few activities that highlight the differences between Terrie and me like taking a trip together.

The first difference is in the way we prepare. Terrie begins weeks in advance with multiple trips to the store for needed supplies. I generally pack the night before. (I, too, make trips to the store, but it is usually after I arrive at my destination and discover how much I forgot.)

The next difference is in how we pack. I usually bring one midsize suitcase and a computer bag carry-on. Terrie normally brings a midsize suitcase, a large suitcase, a wheeled carry-on, and a shoulder bag. And, of course, I carry all of it.

This difference in our packing became especially significant to me last summer at the airport in Edinburgh when Terrie's suitcase was twenty-eight pounds overweight—a fact we discovered while checking in.

The airline attendant directed us to a nearby metal table, which happened to be directly in the view of the winding line of people still waiting to check in. There in the presence of a couple hundred people, we had to open her suitcase, begin pulling her items out—souvenirs, clothes, shoes, personal items—and transfer them to my suitcase, all the while guessing on the weight of both of our bags.

Even after all of our shifting, with just forty minutes before our international flight left, I had to run to an airport shop and buy a $70 suitcase and check an extra bag.

A third area of difference between us in travel is our approach to the trip, especially if it is a vacation. Terrie's idea is we sleep a little into the morning, enjoy a late breakfast, walk through a park, enjoy scenery, and have a little lunch. After lunch, we rest a little more, have dinner, and maybe finish the day playing a game together.

My idea is to rise early with an already prepared map in my hand highlighting the top five to ten most picturesque or historical places. The lunches, rest, or games are all secondary to working through this list. In my approach to travel, you must have a map, you must have a plan, and you must conquer.

Over the years, we've learned to compromise and have grown in our sensitivity to one another. We may visit one less museum for an evening game, and Terrie may give up a gelato for an extra site from my map. We're still a work in progress for sure, but we're growing.

And when it comes to the journey of marriage, growth is what matters most. I think most of us begin marriage with the idea that marriage itself is a destination. Although we don't actually express it, we approach our wedding with the subconscious expectation that once we pull away in our rental car with cans clanging off the bumper, we are finally "there." From here on out, we assume, we'll be free to enjoy the incredible destination of "marriage" with our new spouse.

But along the way, perhaps even on our honeymoon, we discover that as wonderful as marriage may be, it's more of a journey than it is a destination. Rather than being an island of unending bliss and nonstop fulfillment, it's like a long road trip—the kind of trip where you're excited for the destination, love the memories along the way, and sometimes get annoyed with aspects of the journey.

After thirty-six years of marriage, however, I can tell you that while marriage is a long journey, it is the kind of journey that actually gets better the longer you're on it.

If you are reading this book as a pre-wedding resource, you probably don't believe me. You wonder how marriage could possibly get any better than what you envision for the first few months of your new life together—daily strolls into the sunset, alternating making each other breakfast in bed, and romantic evenings of paradisiacal joy. This is the stuff of marriage, right?

If, on the other hand, you're reading this book as a last-ditch effort to save your marriage, you may be convinced that marriage gets worse over time. No more daydreaming of strolls into the sunset for you—you can hardly stand to be together in the same room. You don't see marriage as an incredible journey; you see it as a terrible trick that got you trapped as a lifelong travel partner with someone you don't particularly like to be around.

I won't pretend that every day of our marriage has been filled with heart-eye emojis and nonstop romance. The early euphoria of newlyweds does settle into real life routines and challenges, yet some of our best experiences on this journey have been found in those real life moments as we have seen and received God's grace through each other. So although no marriage has *only* the kinds of moments you want to post on social media, when the journey is shared by two people who desire to walk in God's ways and are determined to stay faithful to one another, they can be wonderful years that get better with each anniversary.

As we've experienced ourselves and shared with others throughout over three decades of pastoral ministry, a great marriage—like a great travel experience—doesn't just happen. It takes a plan and a willingness to move in the direction of that plan. That is what this book is about—a biblically-focused guide to help you invest in the areas that make for an amazing journey together.

WHERE WE'RE HEADED

When we had the opportunity several years ago to go to the Holy Land with our adult children, I wanted to be sure that all of us fully absorbed every aspect of this trip. This was too significant of a trip to simply show up and hope we enjoyed it.

I planned a big family dinner for a couple weeks before we were to leave. At the dinner, I gave everyone a three-ring binder with notes I had compiled about the trip. There was an itinerary, complete with notes on the historic and biblical significance of each site, and I included research regarding protocol for travel in Israel and at the various places we would be. I even made a slide show to aid the discussion.

Our kids laugh about this family dinner and the over-the-top preparation that went into it. But they also acknowledge that it *did* help them glean more from the journey.

In a sense, this chapter is like those three-ring binders. Over the next several pages, although we will be looking at a passage that may be familiar to you, we want to pull truths from it that will set a direction we will refer to throughout the rest of this book.

After all, the journey of marriage is designed by God to be amazing and profound. This is not the kind of trip you should expect to just coast through and hope you end up somewhere you like. We want you to experience everything good that God intended when He created marriage.

And God did create marriage to be awesome. In the actual words of Genesis, He made it "very good." Take a moment to read about the very first wedding in history:

> *And the LORD God said, It is not good that the man should be alone; I will make him an help meet for him. And out of the ground the LORD God formed every beast of the field, and every fowl of the air; and brought them unto Adam to see what he would call*

them: and whatsoever Adam called every
living creature, that was the name thereof.
And Adam gave names to all cattle, and to
the fowl of the air, and to every beast of the
field; but for Adam there was not found an
help meet for him.

And the LORD *God caused a deep sleep*
to fall upon Adam, and he slept: and he took
one of his ribs, and closed up the flesh instead
thereof; And the rib, which the LORD *God*
had taken from man, made he a woman, and
brought her unto the man. And Adam said,
This is now bone of my bones, and flesh of my
flesh: she shall be called Woman, because she
was taken out of Man. Therefore shall a man
leave his father and his mother, and shall
cleave unto his wife: and they shall be one flesh.

—GENESIS 2:18–24

This passage is so significant that it is referenced no
less than four times in the New Testament, including by
Jesus Himself.[1] There is so much truth packed into these
few verses—truths about God, marriage, building a God-
honoring marriage, and loving your spouse. But if we learn
nothing else from this passage, we see that although God
designed marriage with purposes not fully disclosed in this
passage, He did it, in part, with Adam and Eve's pleasure
in mind.

It was *God* who said Adam shouldn't be alone. It was *God* who made Eve. It was *God* who brought them together in a sacred union that would bring mutual satisfaction. Marriage originated in the heart of God who perfectly designed it and beautifully created it.

As the originator of marriage, God set how it is supposed to function. It is through discovering and following His plan from the pages of Scripture that we experience maximum enjoyment from marriage.

YOUR TRAVEL PARTNER

Marriage, at its deepest level, is a friendship. I don't mean this in the way that awkward teens say "Can we be 'just friends'?" but in the sense that God designed marriage to give the companionship and completion which He created us to need.

It is interesting to note that even before sin entered the world—when Adam had perfect fellowship with God—God said, "It is not good that the man should be alone." This need for a partner, then, wasn't due to any imperfection in Adam but to his created purpose. It is hardwired into our souls to crave companionship; and one of the ways—perhaps the pinnacle way—God designed for that need to be met is through marriage.

This is why it is so important that married couples give careful attention to the relational aspects of marriage—communication, acceptance, conflict resolution, spending quality time together, and many other topics we'll look at together in these pages.

If marriage to you is little more than a partner for sex or someone to pay the bills or a person to enjoy in whatever capacity on an as-needed basis, you are missing the fullness of what God intended the companionship of marriage to be—spiritual, emotional, and physical intimacy of two lives. It is an interlocking of souls.

God made Adam and Eve to perfectly complete each other. We see this even in the words used in Genesis to identify them. The Hebrew word for *man* is *Ish*. But the word that translates as *woman, Isha,* literally means "from man." This explains Adam's statement, "she shall be called Woman, because she was taken out of Man."

Notice the depth of the relationship God designed for marriage as you again read Genesis 2:24: "Therefore shall a man leave his father and his mother, and shall cleave unto his wife: *and they shall be one flesh.*"

One flesh. This isn't natural. A bond this close is a miracle of God.

HOW TO GET THERE FROM HERE

Does what we have seen of God's design for marriage sound unrealistic? Unattainable? After all, how do you get there from where you are now?

Some people seem to have an intuitive sense of direction and ability to find their way around. I (Terrie) have always said that if my husband was not a pastor, he would make a great tour guide because he is not only good at researching and describing the historical significance of sites, but he is also very good at navigating his way around unfamiliar places.

One of my favorite stories of needing directions, however, took place in New York City when we were with another couple also visiting from out of state. We ladies were in the back seat and the men in the front with my husband driving. After some time, it became apparent that they didn't know their way. Finally, after several obviously wrong turns and some pointed hints from the back seat, Paul pulled over at a gas station to ask for directions.

We were relieved and grateful as we watched our husbands talk with another man who was pumping gas. We could tell from his gestures that he felt confident to give directions, and we could see our husbands nodding as they listened.

But when they got back in the car and shut the doors, they turned to one another and asked the same question in unison: "What did he say?"

It turned out that their informant didn't speak very clear English, and while they both pretended to understand, they hoped the other was really getting it. It took more driving and another stop for directions before we were pointed in the right direction.

Thankfully, the instructions God gives for forming the bond He designed for marriage are clear and straightforward from the first mention of marriage in Scripture. Genesis 2:24 describes three aspects of it, and you can remember these with three rhyming words: leaving, cleaving, weaving.

Leaving

"Therefore shall a man leave his father and his mother...."

Considering the context in which this was first stated, the verse is almost comical. After all, Adam *had* no father or mother to leave. Yet this truth is so foundational to a healthy marriage that God included His "leaving instruction" in the record of the first marriage.

The word *leave* comes from the Hebrew word *azab* and means "to loosen, i.e., relinquish." It speaks of a severance. When a man and woman join in marriage, they are establishing a new identity together, and that necessitates leaving their previous individual identities—physically and emotionally.

We often illustrate this in weddings with the unity candle, as the bride and groom use the two candles lit previously in the ceremony to light the single unity candle and then blow out the individual candles. This symbol doesn't mean that the bride and groom have lost personal identity, but that they are leaving their previous family units and their identities as separate from each other to create a new home in which they are inseparably joined.

This leaving—not just the physical leaving, but the emotional leaving as well—is vital to a new marriage. Couples need to leave behind the expectations and emotional baggage of the past—how her father treated her mother and the expectations his father had for his mother. Even in homes with a strong, healthy marriage, and especially in homes with a troubled or broken marriage, there are pieces of the past that need to be left behind.

In premarital counseling, I encourage couples to identify and then refuse to carry into their marriage the anger, indifference, noncommunication, and other habits that may have been part of their upbringing. Even after marriage as you detect those trends in your life, remember there are some things that must be left behind to create a strong, healthy relationship. I'm of course not suggesting that you should forget your past or turn your back on your family. In fact, you should learn what you can from your parents and do all you can to maintain a strong relationship with them. But at some point, you need to recognize the distinction between *learning* and *leaving*.

Cleaving

"…and shall cleave unto his wife.…"

God designed marriage to be a relationship where partners cleave to one another—like glue, they are inseparable. This word speaks of total acceptance and unconditional love and respect for one another.

When God brought Eve to Adam, his immediate response was full and unconditional acceptance: "And Adam said, This is now bone of my bones, and flesh of my flesh…" (Genesis 2:23). This is every woman's dream—that a man would give her this absolute acceptance. And truth be told, it's a man's dream too.

The story is told of a young bride who, on the day of her wedding, was almost paralyzed by fear that she would mess the ceremony up. Just before her dad walked her down the aisle, he told her, "Look, it's simple. There are just three words you need to remember: *aisle, altar, hymn.* You walk down the *aisle,* pause at the *altar,* and the soloist will sing a *hymn.* From there, the pastor will take over the ceremony. Just remember: *aisle, altar, hymn.*"

The bride remembered what her father said as they walked in together. Over and over in her mind she repeated the words: *aisle, altar, hymn. Aisle, altar, hymn.*

And that, as the story goes, is how women go into marriage with the idea that *I'll alter him.*

Truthfully, many people do approach marriage with the idea that they can change their spouse after they are married. After marriage, most spouses find out that changing another person is not only impossible, but attempting to do so is damaging to their relationship. The instruction of Genesis 2 for a couple to *cleave* to one another includes that we accept and love our spouse for who they are.

Total acceptance and unconditional love are not common in today's relationships. Some would even say it is impossible or foolish. The world believes that couples who stay married fifty, sixty, and seventy years must have been perfect for each other—that their success is rooted in the fact that they were two lucky people who found their soulmates and that the rest of us mortals are foolish to insist on cleaving to one another during times of pain or difficulty.

The world is wrong. Marriage, as God designed it, carries a commitment to cleave—to hold onto your spouse. It is a decision you make when you exchange marriage vows with one another and a decision you keep every day of your lives as you freely give acceptance and refuse to let your hearts wander from one another.

Weaving

"…and they shall be one flesh."

This is where the real work of marriage comes in. It is the intertwining of lives that happens over time. And it is the stuff of marriage.

Several weeks ago, I had the privilege of preaching with Dr. Bobby Roberson, a man who has pastored the same church for sixty years in the state of North Carolina. His wife of sixty-one years, Jackie, went to Heaven about a year and a half ago. He wept as he shared how he missed her still. You could just sense that part of *him* was missing in Jackie being gone. Over time, the Robersons' lives had so woven together that they *were each other*.

In one sense, this becoming "one flesh" is to take place on your wedding day. Hebrews 13:4 tells us, "Marriage is honourable in all, and the bed undefiled…." Marital intimacy is a gift of God, the physical celebration of oneness and unity. But the weaving of two lives together is more than physical. It takes place through daily decisions to pursue your spouse's heart, to draw near to each other in acceptance, to entwine your lives around each other.

Weaving in the fullest sense cannot happen without spiritual growth together. When you take two lives who are committed to one another and are daily drawing nearer to the Lord, there is an intertwining of souls that is constantly being strengthened by the power of God. This isn't the result of one day, but of habits carried out day after day—praying together, reading God's Word together, worshiping together, serving together, and living out God's will with one another.

Many couples don't pursue this intimacy. Each partner hopes for his or her personal gratification, but neither has a real long-term goal of weaving their lives together. This, however, is the end goal that God has in mind for marriage—two lives intertwined with one another as they grow together in Him.

THE JOURNEY OF A LIFETIME

Marriage—this wonderful melding of two lives, was designed to last. When Jesus taught on marriage, He highlighted this truth by quoting from and expounding on Genesis 2:

> *And he answered and said unto them, Have ye not read, that he which made them at the beginning made them male and female, And said, For this cause shall a man leave father and mother, and shall cleave to his wife: and they twain shall be one flesh? Wherefore they are no more twain, but one flesh.* ***What therefore God hath joined together, let not man put asunder.***—MATTHEW 19:4–6

Marriage, by God's design, is to be one man plus one woman for one lifetime. This is why at a wedding, couples exchange *vows*, not signed contracts. When Terrie and I purchased our first home several years after we were married, we signed a mortgage contract with the bank. This document included many contingencies, noting that if either party defaulted in specific aspects of the agreement, the other was released from their obligation to the contract. But marriage is different. When we were married, we didn't exchange contracts; we exchanged vows.

At your wedding, you too, likely repeated vows similar to these:

> I, ____, take thee, _____
>> to have and to hold....
>> from this day forward...
>> for better, for worse...
>> for richer, for poorer...
>> in sickness and in health...
>> to love and to cherish...
>> 'til death do us part.

Marriage is not a 50/50 proposition in which each can expect the other to carry half the load and assume if the other doesn't keep their half, they are free to drop their own. Rather, marriage is a 100/100 percent commitment in which each spouse promises to wholly give themselves to the other regardless of how well the other is doing.

We know from the Bible that while God loves all people (John 3:16, 2 Peter 3:9), He hates divorce.

> *Yet ye say, Wherefore? Because the* LORD *hath been witness between thee and the wife of thy youth, against whom thou hast dealt treacherously: yet is she thy companion, and the wife of thy covenant. And did not he make one? Yet had he the residue of the spirit. And wherefore one? That he might seek a godly seed. Therefore take heed to your spirit, and let none deal treacherously against the wife of his youth. For the* LORD, *the God of Israel, saith that he hateth putting away: for one covereth violence with his garment, saith the* LORD *of hosts: therefore take heed to your spirit, that ye deal not treacherously.*—MALACHI 2:14–16

If you have suffered through the tragedy of a divorce, you understand better than anyone how painful the severing of a marriage is. My purpose is not to stand in judgment of your past or to make you feel condemned over a situation over which you may not have had control.

But whether or not you have been divorced in the past, I do want to challenge you concerning your current marriage that you would commit to its permanence. God didn't design marriage to be a let's-see-if-we-like-it proposition but a covenant of complete commitment to one another. This foundation of commitment will give you the strength to pursue an ever-deepening relationship and to resist the forces that would try to tear you apart.

iMPERFECT PEOPLE ON A PERFECT JOURNEY

If you're familiar with Genesis, you know that in the chapter directly after Adam and Eve were married, these same two people disobeyed God, and through their disobedience sin and death entered the world. "The Fall," as we commonly refer to it, was so significant that Scripture tells us its effects reverberate throughout creation itself (Romans 8:22), and they certainly touch every aspect of our lives.

Every marriage since—including ours and including yours—has been composed of two sinners. Every obstacle we face in marriage—every misplaced expectation, every fight, every lonely tear, every bitter word, every frustration— is the outcome of the Fall.

So although marriage itself is a perfect journey, the special creation of God, it is undertaken by imperfect people. We enter marriage with a longing to experience all that God created it to be, even if we don't fully understand what that means or that it is God who implanted those desires in our hearts. We undertake this journey as sinners married to sinners, and that makes for a bumpy ride.

But it smooths out. Intricately woven into God's plan is that marriage is a picture of His larger plan to redeem mankind. This is *incredible*. Your marriage is so much bigger than you—than both of you. It's bigger than your hopes and dreams and fears and struggles. It's bigger than the minutiae of your daily routines. It's designed by God to be the harmony of two lives that, by covenant vows to each other, have entered a relationship picturing the love, sacrifice, and commitment of Christ and the church.

Don't miss where this picture comes from: After the Fall, even as God told Adam and Eve the punishment for sin was death—physical and spiritual—and that because of sin they would be banished from the Garden and the presence of a holy God, God graciously promised that He would send a Saviour (Genesis 3:15).

As God who took on human flesh, Jesus offered Himself as the complete substitute for our sin. "The wages of sin is death…" (Romans 6:23). "But God commendeth his love toward us, in that, while we were yet sinners, Christ died for us" (Romans 5:8). Jesus died in our place and offers us the full forgiveness of God as a gift. He promises, "For whosoever shall call upon the name of the Lord shall be saved" (Romans 10:13).[2]

And then, what we only see in part in the Old Testament is revealed in the New Testament as a "mystery" which was embedded since the beginning of time into God's purpose—that marriage would be a picture of the love Christ has for the church.

> *For this cause shall a man leave his father and mother, and shall be joined unto his wife, and they two shall be one flesh. This is a great mystery: but I speak concerning Christ and the church.*— EPHESIANS 5:31–32

This is why Satan so fiercely attacks marriage—it is the visible representation of the redemption he hates. And this is also why Christian couples in particular must be committed to following God's plan for marriage. God's plan is not only the best in terms of our happiness, but, as Christians, we have an added commitment to bring glory to God by reflecting the love of Christ in our marriages.

Even if your spouse does not know the Lord or you feel you are the only one who desires to make your marriage better reflect the love of Christ, God can use your commitment to receive and give His love to strengthen your relationship with your spouse and to bring glory to Himself. As you read this book, you may be tempted to think, "Well, that could work for others, but it couldn't work for me." But when you remember the big picture of Christ's love showing through you, it adds perspective and gives strength to invest regardless of your spouse's immediate responses.

After all, the fact that God entrusts any of us imperfect people to live out the perfect picture of His love is nothing short of amazing.

BECAUSE WE ARE NOT THERE YET

Terrie and I had been married about a year and a half when we were offered a free trip to Hawaii. I was still in Bible college, with Terrie expecting our first baby. We had no money, so a free trip to Hawaii was like a dream come true.

This was a timeshare promotional package, which meant we had to listen to a sales pitch upon arrival. But it also meant that if we would listen to additional sales promos every morning, we got "free" daily excursions. You better believe we did it, too! Ninety minutes is a small price to pay for a ride in a glass bottom boat or a free rental car for the day.

The hotel was nicer than anything we had ever stayed in. It included a gourmet breakfast, which took care of one meal each day. The peanut butter and bread we brought in our suitcase helped with another meal. The pineapple pickers were on strike, so for one dollar we could go into the field and pick three pineapples, which gave us our third meal.

You might think that all this strategizing and planning and sales pitch listening would make our vacation less enjoyable. Actually, although we've had the opportunity to go to Hawaii several times since, we've never had more fun there than during that first vacation where we worked so hard to enjoy it. The effort we had to invest increased our anticipation and experience.

Many couples want marriage to be like a luxury vacation that costs nothing and requires nothing of them. They assume that good marriages just happen and struggling marriages are the result of incompatibility.

Yet, nobody assumes this in relation to any other area of life. We work hard to develop skills, to advance in a career, to perfect a hobby, even to plan a vacation. Good marriages also take *work*. They require the purposeful pursuit of one another's heart, the willingness to give and receive total acceptance and unconditional love, and a commitment to oneness for a lifetime.

No couple has "arrived" in their marriage. We're not there yet; you're not there yet. But we are enjoying the journey. And we invite you to do the same.

(above) Enjoying a beautiful fall day in New England.

(right) Stopping for a break from sightseeing—we're both learning to enjoy both breaks and activity as we journey together.

From 1980 until today, from Southern California to London, there is no one I would rather be with than you.

TWO

iT LOOKED DiFFERENT iN THE PiCTURE

Expectations

"I'm taking you on a vacation to *paradise*." Those were my dad's exact words at the family meeting that included all of my immediate family and our spouses. "The exchange rate is so good right now that you can eat steak and lobster every night," he continued.

He passed around brochures for Rosarito, Mexico, replete with stunning views of the ocean and highlighting a full range of activities. The one that caught Terrie's and my attention was horseback riding. The picture showed a lady with long, flowing hair galloping across the beach on a beautiful horse. We determined right then that horseback riding was the activity for us, and we eagerly planned and packed for this vacation.

Let's just say Rosarito was not what we had anticipated—not what the pamphlets had pictured at all. First, our hotel was not the one in the brochure. It wasn't even in the same neighborhood. Second, although the exchange rate was good, the prices were set for tourists. No steak and lobster for us.

One day on this trip, we saw a burro with white zebra stripes painted on it harnessed to a wooden cart. There was a sign that said, "Color pictures $5." Danielle was a baby at the time, and we decided it would be fun to have a family picture on a cart behind the zebra-burro. I paid, we got in the cart, and all smiled for the picture. The man who owned the burro developed it right there and gave it to us—a black and white print.

"But I thought this was supposed to be a color picture," I said.

"Sí, Señor, it *is* color—*black* and *white*."

This trip wasn't turning out to be quite what we envisioned. We balanced our disappointment, however, by reminding ourselves that at least we could go horseback riding on the beach.

We left bright and early the next morning with visions of ourselves, brilliantly printed in our minds, galloping across the beach on princely horses. When we arrived at the place advertised for horse rentals, we found a limited selection of horses—two. Terrie's horse had only one eye. My horse was well past his retirement years and had to be led. To make matters worse, we couldn't seem to get the boy leading it to understand we wanted to go to the beach. He led us through the streets of Rosarito where his friends surrounded us, asking for money.

When we finally got back to our hotel, we looked again at the picture of the lady galloping across the beach. Apparently that horse had already been rented by the time we arrived. Or maybe it was just a photo prop.

We are wiser now to travel brochures. A photographer can capture a small snapshot that is wildly different from the full experience.

And so it is in marriage. We see snapshots of marriage in other people's lives, on social media, and in culture. From these, we build our own expectations. But we soon discover that our mental images are vastly different from reality.

EXPECTATIONS RUIN RELATIONSHIPS

Sometimes the collision between our expectations and reality may be humorous—at least in hindsight. One of Terrie's early, unspoken expectations of marriage was that I would help around the house. Shortly after we were married, we had invited company over for dinner. I noticed she was stressed with the preparations, and I offered to help. I was pleased with how delighted she was at my offer and silently congratulated myself on my sensitivity and kindness.

Then I rolled up my sleeves and tackled what looked to me like the biggest project—alphabetizing the bookshelf.

Although we both laugh at that incident now, it didn't strike Terrie as funny then. But it was one of our early discoveries of how easily expectations collide in marriage.

It is expectations and misunderstandings like these that set couples up for an ongoing stream of disappointment. In marriage counseling, we almost always find that marital disappointment comes from unrealistic, and often unspoken, expectations spouses have of one another.

We come to marriage with more expectations than we realize—cultural, familial, relational…. There are 1,001 influences from the time we are born until this present moment that shape our perspectives and underlying expectations. Expectations, in fact, are so deeply embedded into our worldview that we rarely consider them as being a topic of discussion. We simply assume everyone else looks at the world just as we do.

Of course, not all expectations are wrong or unreasonable. Marriage itself is built on the expectation that your spouse will honor his or her vows to you. You *want* your spouse to expect that you love and care for him or her. Together, you expect your marriage will grow and that you are both fully committed to it. It's also not wrong to expect that your spouse will follow through on promises or to make promises you want your spouse to believe.

What we're speaking about here are expectations that are built on a spirit of pride or self-thought. They are often unspoken, and they are sometimes unidentified, even when they are our own. If we don't recognize them, we will become embittered toward our spouse because of them.

We see unmet expectations throughout Scripture. Sometimes they were false expectations of God and sometimes unrealistic expectations of others. The psalmist Asaph expected that ungodly people should not experience wealth while he served God and struggled. When his expectations were not met, he almost lost his faith (Psalm 73:1–17). Rachel expected she would have children and blamed her husband Jacob when she didn't (Genesis 30:1). The workers in Jesus' parable expected they would be compensated above what they had been promised. When they weren't, they nursed a grudge (Matthew 20:10–11).

One of the classic accounts of misplaced expectations is in 2 Kings 5 where we find the Syrian captain, Naaman, going to the prophet Elisha to be healed of leprosy. Naaman arrived at Elisha's doorstep with a large entourage, but Elisha simply sent his servant to the door with instructions for Naaman to dip seven times into the muddy Jordan River. Naaman was offended, and he left Elisha's house "in a rage" (anger is a classic indicator of unmet expectations). Notice Naaman's response.

> *But Naaman was wroth, and went away, and said, Behold, I thought, He will surely come out to me, and stand, and call on the name of the LORD his God, and strike his hand over the place, and recover the leper. Are not Abana and Pharpar, rivers of Damascus, better than all the waters of Israel? may I not wash in them, and be clean? So he turned and went away in a rage.*—2 KINGS 5:11–12

Naaman came to Elisha with a full set of unspoken expectations. He expected Elisha would come to him in person, perform an elaborate ceremony, and bring on-the-spot healing. When this didn't happen, Naaman's disappointment turned into anger. It was only the persuasion of Naaman's servants that brought Naaman around to the place where he was willing to let his expectations go and humbly do as the prophet had told him. (And just to not leave you hanging, Naaman did then experience the miraculous healing of God.)

But think about Naaman's initial response: *"Behold, I thought...."* When you hear yourself say, "But I just thought..." that's your clue that you're dealing with unmet expectations. And when you feel the frustration and anger rising, that is another indication that you are responding to unmet expectations.

I've heard many unrealistic expectations over the years. They usually begin with the phrase, "But I thought...." Here are several of the most common:

- **But I thought marriage would make me happy.** It is easy, especially for people who are not yet married or who are struggling in their marriage, to turn marriage into a personal idol, believing that the "perfect spouse" is the answer to any unhappiness in life. This expectation places an incredible pressure on a spouse. No spouse is perfect, and no person can be your single source of happiness. Only Jesus can give you continuing happiness.

  Over the past couple of years, a few people have mentioned to me the big smile and evident joy of one of the ladies who sings in our church choir. What they don't know is that her husband is a Muslim, and that her heart is broken for his salvation. She longs to see him saved and to enjoy spiritual unity as a couple. Yet, even so, she has found her joy in the Lord. Marriage is an awesome gift, but it is not a place to depend on for your happiness.

- **But I thought my spouse would meet all of my needs.** Focusing on your needs can only ruin a marriage.

Every husband has unique needs, as does every wife. Ephesians 5 speaks to the individual nature of each spouse's needs as it commands wives to honor their husbands and husbands to love their wives. But don't miss the obvious—the command to each spouse is to meet the other's needs, not to focus on his or her own needs.

- **But I thought he/she would change after we got married.** Someone once pointed out that a man marries a woman expecting her to never change, and a woman marries a man expecting to change him—and they are both wrong!

  Marrying someone with the expectation they will become a different person after marriage is unreasonable and unfair. Marriage is not a magic change agent that transforms a person. Before you are married, your job is to be sure the person you want to marry is someone you can trust. After marriage, your job is to work to understand and love the person you married.

- **But I thought if I found the right one, marriage would be easy.** Good marriages take effort. It requires real work to understand your spouse and honor and love him or her. A spouse who is passionate about a strong marriage thinks about his or her spouse often and constantly invests in the relationship.

- **But I thought good marriages never struggle.** Actually, most marriages will "hit a wall." Sometimes a couple is surprised by a season of difficulty in their marriage. This faulty expectation leads them to assume then that their marriage is already as good as gone. If, when you encounter such a season, you recognize that every difficulty can be worked through with the grace of God, biblical truth (perhaps including wise counsel), and a determination to strengthen your relationship, you'll get through it—and be stronger for it.

Do you see your thoughts in any of those expectations? If you were to finish this sentence, "But I just thought that he/she would _____," how would you fill in the blank?

THE DOWNHILL PATH TO HAPPINESS

Our flesh tells us that the only way our unfulfilled expectations can be overcome is if our spouse will change and turn those expectations into fulfilled desires. Scripture tells us there is another way.

The journey to happiness in marriage is not one of insisting that your spouse change. It is in learning to change your thoughts by letting the mind of Christ become yours.

> *Let this mind be in you, which was also in Christ Jesus: Who, being in the form of God, thought it not robbery to be equal with God: But made himself of no reputation, and took upon him the form of a servant, and was made in the likeness of men: And being found in fashion as a man, he humbled himself, and became obedient unto death, even the death of the cross.*
> —PHILIPPIANS 2:5–8

These words are convicting to me every time I read them. Interestingly, they come directly after verses about relational unity: "Let nothing be done through strife or vainglory; but in lowliness of mind let each esteem other better than themselves. Look not every man on his own things, but every man also on the things of others" (Philippians 2:3–4).

If you were to take this passage at absolute face value, how do you think it would transform your marriage?

Jesus came to earth with *only* an expectation to serve and sacrifice for others. "For even the Son of man came not to be ministered unto, but to minister, and to give his life a ransom for many" (Mark 10:45). Jesus had no hidden agenda—no "If I serve them, they'll do _____ for me" mentality.

Jesus' humility is a rebuke to our self-centered thought patterns. If you want to transform your thinking toward your spouse, saturate your mind with Philippians 2:3–8. Read it daily. Think on it. Memorize it. Write it out. Let it reprogram your mind from one of expectancy to Christlikeness.

THREE DOWNWARD STEPS TO TAKE EVERY DAY

Our shift in expectations initially takes place in our minds. But at some point, we must take action steps toward our spouse if we are to shift from expecting to serving.

So, what does Philippians 2 living look like in everyday terms? Here are three actions Terrie and I endeavor to take daily:

1. Die to self. When we trust Christ as our Saviour, He gives us a new nature. Second Corinthians 5:17 promises, "Therefore if any man be in Christ, he is a new creature: old things are passed away; behold, all things are become new."

But the habits of our hearts and the temptations of life don't vanish overnight. The Bible calls this continuing pull toward sin "the flesh." *The flesh* is my tendency to satisfy my needs or desires outside the obedience of God. Galatians 5:17 explains, "For the flesh lusteth against the Spirit, and the Spirit against the flesh: and these are contrary the one to the other: so that ye cannot do the things that ye would."

Even as a Christian with the indwelling Holy Spirit of God, I have a terrible tendency to build expectations of what Terrie should do or be for me with myself at the center of them. When I say, "I just thought she would understand my need for _____," that's usually an indication of selfishness. And pride. And discontent. And.... In short, it's fleshliness.

Here's the thing about the flesh: you can't reform it. You can't just "try harder" to have less expectations or to be less selfish. This is why the Apostle Paul wrote, "I die daily" (1 Corinthians 15:31). He wasn't saying that he physically died and miraculously resurrected every day; he was teaching us that the only way to overcome the flesh is to kill it.

In Galatians 2:20, which has become my life verse, Paul expounds on this truth: "I am crucified with Christ: nevertheless I live; yet not I, but Christ liveth in me: and the life which I now live in the flesh I live by the faith of the Son of God, who loved me, and gave himself for me."

This verse echoes a truth that shows up throughout the entire New Testament: as believers, we are "in Christ." The Christian life was never designed to simply be a "get out of hell free" card; it is to be a life of union with Jesus.

Our spiritual relationship to God is that we have the righteousness of Jesus and the ability to allow the life of Jesus to live through us.

But it requires that we choose to die to our fleshly tendencies and desires. Romans 6:11 assures us that as Christians we have the power to do this: "Likewise reckon ye also yourselves to be dead indeed unto sin, but alive unto God through Jesus Christ our Lord."

For me, this dying to self process begins every day as I pray something like this: "Lord, today I die to self. I reckon myself—my tendencies, habits, and selfish expectations—dead because of Your cross and because I am 'in You.' I ask You to live through me—that Your power and truth would dominate my heart and that Your Spirit would guide me today."

I don't recite these words as a memorized prayer every day. But I do make a conscious decision every day to die to self and surrender to let Christ live through me. Sometimes I simply pray the words of Galatians 2:20.

A prayer like this cannot and does not obliterate the temptations that would arise during the day, but it does set my heart in the right direction and prepare me to yield to the Holy Spirit during those in-the-moment temptations to selfishness that will arise all day long.

2. Yield to the Holy Spirit. It is 2:00 in the afternoon, and your wife has asked you *again* if you've heard back on any of the job applications you submitted yesterday. Last time she asked, you told her you'd let her know as soon as you did, which is a pretty clear way of saying, "Please don't ask again." You would expect she would understand that, right?

What do you do in that moment? You could respond in the flesh, which, depending on your personality, may involve anything from raising your voice with an exasperated, cutting answer, to giving the silent treatment, to an all-out shouting fight; or you could, in that moment, listen to the Holy Spirit encouraging you to die to self and give grace.

One of the unique dynamics of the Christian life is that it cannot work without the power of God. The Christian life was never meant to be lived in your own strength, but by the empowering of the Holy Spirit who lives within you. It is no coincidence that the scriptural command to "be filled with the Spirit" (Ephesians 5:18) is the prelude to some of the most direct marriage counsel in the Bible (Ephesians 5:22–33, which we will look at in our next chapter). Being filled with the Spirit is simply the act of surrender to God. It is a decision of faith to yield control of yourself to the Holy Spirit and to the commands of His Word.

Without allowing the Holy Spirit to fill, or to control, your life, your days will be controlled by false expectations and fleshly responses. In stark contrast, the result of being filled with the Spirit is a set of qualities every Christian couple wants to characterize their lives and their marriage: "But the fruit of the Spirit is love, joy, peace, longsuffering, gentleness, goodness, faith, Meekness, temperance: against such there is no law" (Galatians 5:22–23).

We think that if we yield our rights and surrender our expectations to God, we'll be trampled on, made a doormat, be taken advantage of, and lose our identity. But read that list describing the fruit of the Spirit from Galatians 5 again: love, joy, peace, longsuffering, gentleness, goodness, faith, meekness, temperance. Could you use those qualities in your marriage? It's a matter of yielding.

3. Serve your spouse. The only Christlike expectation is the expectation to serve. Think again of Philippians 2 and Christ's humility. Jesus had every right to expect to be served. But He chose instead to serve.

The most practical step you can take to curb unrealistic expectations is to purposefully serve your spouse without expecting anything in return. Look for real, tangible, specific ways to meet your spouse's needs.

The world conditions us to expect. Glossy advertising, consumer-driven marketing, resorts, amusement parks… they all say, "You deserve more; let us give it to you." Yet the world consistently underperforms. The higher our expectations, the less satisfied reality becomes. Only a servant will be pleasantly surprised.

Several years ago, Terrie and I were in Italy with our son and daughter-in-law, Larry and Ashley, and Ashley's parents, Ernie and Lori Baydo. Larry had just been through two major surgeries followed by months of chemo treatments for cancer. Toward the outset of Larry's treatments, I had told him once he got through them, we would go anywhere he would like together. Larry had been studying the life of Paul and wanted an opportunity to travel to the locations where he was used of God to preach the gospel, especially Mars Hill in Athens. While in that part of the world, we took a mini tour tracing the footsteps of the apostle Paul throughout the Mediterranean region. This trip became one of the most enriching trips for all of us relating to Bible study and teaching and preaching.

At one point on this trip, we were at a restaurant in Milan, Italy, and really up against the clock to catch a train to our next destination. When I told the waiter that we were in a hurry and needed our food quickly, he responded with a phrase that indicated his desire to help. His words became our motto for the rest of the trip and a favorite saying in our family since: "I want to make you happy."

What could happen in your marriage if you adopted this phrase as your motto? "I want to make you happy."

What if, instead of expecting to be made happy, you made it your number one desire to make your spouse happy? Have you given thought to what your spouse's needs are? Are you willing to set aside your own needs and expectations to meet those?

In the excellent book *His Needs, Her Needs,* author Willard Harley, Jr.[1] highlights five semi-corresponding needs of husbands and wives that he has discovered through extensive counseling:

His Needs	Her Needs
Sexual Fulfillment	Affection
Recreational Companionship	Intimate Conversation
Physical Attractiveness	Honesty and Openness
Domestic Support	Financial Support
Admiration	Family Commitment

Remember that Christlike servanthood isn't serving with the expectation of getting. *(If I make his favorite meal, he will become more verbally communicative. If I buy her flowers, she will be more physically responsive.)* It's not manipulative. It is serving with the expectation of serving. That's it.

How do you know what your spouse's needs are? Getting to know your spouse and learning to anticipate his or her needs is one way. Another is to simply ask, "What can I do today to help you?" In fact, that is a tremendous question to ask every day.

LOVE IS A CHOICE

If you remain married for longer than five minutes, you will experience unmet expectations. It's part of life, and it's definitely part of marriage.

The world conditions us to believe that love is fueled by a spouse being "everything I ever dreamed." When we discover our spouse is *not* everything we dreamed (and no spouse is), we have two choices: we can become disillusioned, or we can choose to love unconditionally and serve sacrificially.

The feeling of being "in love" comes easily when all of my expectations are being met. But true love, selfless love, requires the hard work of discovering what my wife needs, selflessly serving her, and having the personal discipline and commitment to do that again and again and again.

This is the kind of love described in 1 Corinthians 13:

> *Charity suffereth long, and is kind; charity envieth not; charity vaunteth not itself, is not puffed up, Doth not behave itself unseemly, seeketh not her own, is not easily provoked, thinketh no evil; Rejoiceth not in iniquity, but rejoiceth in the truth;*

Beareth all things, believeth all things,
hopeth all things, endureth all things.
—1 CORINTHIANS 13:4–7

This kind of love involves real choices. It wasn't hard when I was dating Terrie to be late for work because time got away from me while we were spending googly-eyed hours together. (Neither was it hard for my employer to suggest he would let me go if it happened again.) But, I'll be honest, after we were married and Terrie was in bed sick, I did find it hard to do the dishes. Yet, doing the dishes was more loving than staring into each other's eyes. The first was a self-satisfying love; the second was self-sacrificing love. The first was immaturity; the second grew our relationship.

Choosing to serve has a powerful way of releasing our expectations. But it gets even better. It positions us for grace. I don't know of any Christian spouse who wouldn't agree that what their marriage needs more than anything is God's grace. It's what Terrie and I constantly need. It's what you need. And it comes through humility—the humility that submits and serves: "...Yea, all of you be subject one to another, and be clothed with humility: for God resisteth the proud, and giveth grace to the humble" (1 Peter 5:5).

Is choosing to serve when you don't "feel" love a sterile way to live? Is it dead love? Empty of meaning? Not at all. Because service begins with sacrifice, it makes room for the deepest feelings imaginable.

It is servant-based love that allows you to look back at the self-centered picture you originally had of marriage and laugh. For one, you realize that marriage isn't a ready-made photograph. It is a picture that you paint together—day by day, choice by choice, with brushstrokes of service.

And *this* picture—the one that you paint together—turns out to be even better than the travel brochure snapshot you had in your mind. It's real. And it's painted with grace.

Hikers have the right of way

(above) Terrie with the one-eyed horse

(left) In Milan, Italy, waiting for our "I want to make you happy" server

THREE

PAYiNG WiTH FOREiGN CURRENCY

Needs

For all its adventure, international travel includes a deceptively tricky detail—foreign currency.

You think it will be simple. You even download this awesome app on your phone that will do the work for you. Or maybe the exchange rate is so easily rounded to the nearest dollar that you feel confident you've got this.

Don't be fooled. The greatest challenge is not the math; it is that you will *forget* to calculate the exchange.

Actually, before credit cards began offering built-in currency conversion services, I was more successful with foreign currency. When we'd arrive in a foreign country,

I'd exchange our American dollars for the currency of that country. The very fact that I was dealing with pesos, yuan, euro, or pounds forced me to think through the conversion before each purchase. But this is not the case anymore where foreign businesses accept American credit cards. I simply pay with my card, and the credit card company makes the conversion for me.

A few years ago, while on a layover in London, Terrie and I had a day to rest and shop. As we walked along Oxford Street, I stopped to look at a pair of shoes. They were expensive, but I needed shoes, and these were a good brand I knew would hold up well. We decided they'd be a great way to remember the trip on a daily basis, so we bit the bullet and purchased them.

Back home a few weeks later, the credit card statement came in the mail. My jaw dropped as I read it, realizing that back in London I had forgotten the currency exchange rate. I had paid 150 percent of what I had already thought was a high price for that crazy pair of shoes.

I still wear the shoes, and they still remind me of awesome memories with Terrie in London. But every now and then, as I put them on, I wonder how I could have been so foolish as to forget to convert from British pounds to American dollars when I was shopping.

Currency can be difficult to understand. For instance, at the time of this writing, one American dollar equals

0.82 British pounds, 1.72 German marks, 6.92 Chinese yuan, 50.26 Philippine pesos, or 66.50 Indian rupees. If you don't study the exchange rates before you get to a country, it's very easy to get taken advantage of. And if you forget to calculate the exchange rates when you are making a purchase, you may end up spending a significantly different amount than you anticipated.

In marriage, "heart conversion" is a lot like currency conversion. When you think about it, marriage is the perfect scenario for misunderstandings. And it's not because I'm right and she's wrong—but because I forget to convert the real currency of my heart into the real currency of Terrie's heart.

Does that sound confusing? Foreign currency is like that.

Think about it this way: For all the *sameness* that attracted you and your spouse together, there is this pesky fact that the overriding attraction was rooted in what makes you different—man versus woman.

Actually, the fact that there is a distinction between male and female is critical to what marriage is. We understand this on a theological level, but we often forget it on a relational level. We instinctively know that men and women are different, but we forget that those differences are deeper than biological. They have to do with how we think, feel, respond, and with the deepest needs of our hearts. On the surface, some of these differences are easily explained by personality types, backgrounds, or life experiences. But I'm talking about something deeper—something that God embedded into the very makeup of men and women.

DiFFERENT CURRENCiES

There are four main passages in the New Testament that address both husbands and wives in the same passage.[1] Interestingly, three of these highlight the differences in roles and responsibilities between a husband and a wife in marriage. Also, in all three of these passages, God repeats a specific instruction to wives and a specific instruction to husbands. I believe that these instructions highlight the greatest needs of both.

> *Nevertheless let every one of you in particular so love his wife even as himself; and the wife see that she reverence her husband.*—EPHESIANS 5:33

> *Wives, submit yourselves unto your own husbands, as it is fit in the Lord. Husbands, love your wives, and be not bitter against them.*—COLOSSIANS 3:18–19

> *Likewise, ye wives, be in subjection to your own husbands....Likewise, ye husbands, dwell with them according to knowledge,*

giving honour unto the wife, as unto the
weaker vessel...—1 PETER 3:1, 7

The verbiage is a little different in each passage, but at the heart of each is an instruction to wives to give respect and a yielded spirit to their husbands and an instruction to husbands to give tender love to their wives.

Wives, respect; husbands, love.

From our own experience and from over thirty years of marriage counseling, I can tell you that these two commands directly address the basic needs of husbands and wives.

It is the universal need of wives to *feel* loved. Marriage, of course, is built on committed love. So I'm not implying that husbands *don't* need or want love. (They absolutely do.) But women need assurances of love—they need their husbands to express love tenderly and frequently

And it is the universal need of husbands to *feel* respected. Once again, every human being needs and deserves respect. But men have a deep *need* for respect. In the same way that a wife needs her husband to express sacrificial love, a husband needs his wife to express committed respect.

Interestingly, these needs correspond with the biblical roles of men and women in marriage. Husbands are to provide leadership and are commanded to nurture and cherish their wives (Ephesians 5:23–29). Thus a wife giving respect to her husband enables him to fulfill his God-given role. Similarly, wives are to support their husbands by following their leadership and demonstrating a peaceful spirit (1 Peter 3:1–5). Thus, a husband freely and frequently demonstrating tender love to his wife provides the security she needs to fulfill her role.

I've often illustrated these two needs to couples in marital counseling by asking two questions: First I ask the wife, "If you had to choose between your husband telling and showing you that he loves you or him telling and showing you that he respects you, would you choose love or respect?" One hundred percent of the time, the answer is "love." Then I ask the husband, "If you had to choose between your wife telling and showing you that she loves you or her telling and showing you that she respects you, would you choose love or respect?" One hundred percent of the time, the husband answers, "respect."

Of course, in a healthy marriage, no one has to make a choice between love and respect. Both spouses give both to each other. But the specific commands of God related to marriage highlight the greatest need each spouse has as well as what tends to be the greatest challenge for each spouse to give.

Because respect is a great need in my life that Terrie can supply, sometimes I assume it is her greatest need as then parted ways. Cabo San Lucas is a big city with many hotels. I did not expect to see them again.

Twenty minutes later, we were in the check-in line at our hotel, and who should we see in front of us but the exact same couple. Once again, we chatted. And once again, after we left for our respective rooms, Terrie and I reminded each other that this was a big hotel, and really there were few chances for interaction the rest of our time there.

That evening at dinner, just after we were seated, we looked up to see this couple who asked if we minded if they sat with us.

"Sure," I said, and I really tried to mean it.

It was then that the husband told us, "We're having incredible problems in our marriage. Her dad sent us here to get away and hopefully work our difficulties out. This week is our last effort to save our marriage. Can you help us?"

No pressure, right?

We spent two hours that evening offering marriage counseling.

For the next five days we either saw them somewhere or they found us. And we spent, on average, two hours per day trying to help them.

The last morning we were there, I grabbed my sunglasses, ball cap, book, and a chair and told Terrie, "I am going to find a private spot by the ocean and read. If I

well. I find it more natural to convey respect to Terrie than I do sacrificial love. I also tend to feel more insulted when I do not perceive her conveying respect to me. Similarly, it's more natural for Terrie to show affection than respect and to feel more hurt when I show respect rather than affection.[2] Perhaps this is why God instructs men to sacrificially love their wives and wives to specifically respect their husbands.

Neither love nor respect is more valuable than the other, nor is one spouse more worthy of one than the other. These are two currencies of the same value; they simply happen to be two different currencies.

HEIRS TOGETHER

I think my favorite description of marriage is found in 1 Peter 3:7: "…as being heirs together of the grace of life." In Christ, the husband and wife have equal value and equal standing before God. They are heirs together of God's grace. It is this togetherness in grace that is one of the greatest joys of a Christian marriage.

So when we speak of differences in needs, responsibilities, and roles between a husband and a wife in marriage, we are not talking about a difference in intrinsic value. We are simply referring to the fact that differences between men and women, husbands and wives, go deeper than the obvious surface differences.

As humans, we all have equal value as being made in the image of God (Genesis 1:27). As believers in Christ, we have equal standing with God as heirs of His grace. But in marriage, we have varying needs and responsibilities. A good marriage is one in which both spouses learn to understand and fulfill the needs of the other.

NEEDS AND ROLES

Our culture has, by and large, resisted the roles that God built into marriage, claiming that they are stereotypical or in some way oppressive. Whatever they may be, they are not oppressive. They are God's design for the gift He created.

Consider the manual in your car. If you're like me, you keep it in the glove box and refer to it only seldomly, like when you can't figure out how the sound system works. But when you do refer to the manual, you never assume that the car manufacturer wrote it with malicious intent to make the car less pleasant for you to drive. You assume that following the manual will make your car last longer and your experience in it better.

So it is with marriage. God has called a husband to provide loving, servant leadership in the home, and He has called a wife to give honor and submission to her husband. Following the roles that God embedded into the creation of marriage is integral to our enjoyment of it. Understanding

these roles and learning how to communicate love and respect to one another is crucial to having spiritual unity and emotional teamwork in your relationship.

We were confronted with just how important these needs and roles are early in our ministry.

We've had several times throughout the years when we have hit a wall of physical fatigue and knew that we needed rest to be able to continue serving. This was perhaps the first of these times.

It was wintertime, and we decided that if we were going to get away for a couple days, we wanted to go to a warmer climate. (Although we live in Southern California, we are in the high desert region. At 2,400 feet elevation, Lancaster gets cold, bitter winds in the winter.) We found a great deal for five days in Cabo San Lucas, Mexico. This was an ideal location because we knew we would have solitude and would be free to relax, unwind, and just enjoy each other. We booked our tickets, found a sitter for our children, and anticipated five glorious days.

The flight from Los Angeles was less than two hours. We held hands on the plane and as we landed and walked to our baggage claim.

At baggage claim, we were surprised to see a couple from our church. I suggested to Terrie that we should walk over and be friendly to them. We greeted one another and

don't get some down time on this trip, I'll go back just as exhausted as when we left."

It hadn't been ten minutes after I had settled in to my secluded spot when there was a tap on my shoulder. You guessed it—it was the husband of this couple. "Pastor, we've been here for five days, and she hasn't even touched me. What am I supposed to do?"

The root of their problem related to a disregard for the God-given roles in marriage. She had an executive job in the fashion district of Los Angeles (about an hour and a half commute, on a good day, from where they lived) and made significantly more money than he did. Because she made more than him, she treated him poorly, not giving him respect. He, in turn, treated her dismissively, not giving her love or leadership. In most cases, when a wife works more or earns more than her husband, the role of who is the main provider for the family reverses, and a man resents that. In this case, it was as if her being the leader in income gave both of them the (unspoken) sense that she should also be the leader of the home.

We pleaded with them to focus on the spiritual aspects of their relationship rather than the material. We counseled them that if she intended to keep that job, she would need to, in the grace of the Holy Spirit, practice a deferring, submissive heart toward her husband and that he would need to practice a spirit of gratitude and gentle love toward her. I explained to him that he should still provide spiritual leadership and direction for the home.

Unfortunately, this couple did not follow the biblical counsel we gave. Shortly after this trip, they stopped coming to church and soon after divorced.

Their story is one of too many couples who want their spouse to give in the way God instructs in Ephesians 5, but each is unwilling to *be* the giving spouse. In fact, in all these years of preaching and teaching from Ephesians 5, although many people have told me they didn't like what the Bible says about their *own* role in marriage, I've never had one person think the *other* spouse's role was unimportant. While a husband may struggle to be a loving servant leader, he wants his wife to respect him. Similarly, while a wife may struggle to follow her husband's leadership, she wants him to freely communicate affectionate love. It is when each spouse will embrace and fulfill their own roles that the other's deepest needs are met and the marriage flourishes. (And it is neglecting these roles that makes the marriage deteriorate.)

Remember, the goal in understanding these roles is not selfish—so your spouse can do a better job relating to you—but you must know how to give grace and love to one another in the currency that they most readily use and understand.

So let's look at these currencies more closely and then examine how to make currency conversions in marriage. For the sake of clarity, we'll be looking primarily from Ephesians 5 but will reference other passages as well.

THE CURRENCY OF RESPECT
(What a Husband Most Needs and Understands)

> *Wives, submit yourselves unto your own husbands, as unto the Lord. For the husband is the head of the wife, even as Christ is the head of the church: and he is the saviour of the body. Therefore as the church is subject unto Christ, so let the wives be to their own husbands in every thing.*—EPHESIANS 5:22–24

That this passage begins with instruction to the wife underscores the importance of her role. When either spouse fulfills their role regardless of the other's obedience to their own role, it can make a tremendous difference in a marriage. But when a wife gets the ball in motion, it has an even more powerful effect because it changes the whole spirit of the relationship.

The Greek word translated *submit* in Ephesians 5:22 is *hupotasso*. It means "to arrange under, to subordinate, to subject one's self." Notice the decision involved. This is a *voluntary* submission, a willing choice.

I like what Joyce Rogers wrote in relation to the wife's role in marriage: "To prove submission is a wonderful concept, Jesus became the ultimate illustration of its validity. Although He was coequal and coeternal with the Father, He was completely submissive to the Father's will." Superiority or inferiority do not even enter into the equation. A godly wife chooses to submit to and honor her husband's leadership as an expression of her trust in the Lord.

But she also does it as an expression of love to her husband. Perhaps in part because of the responsibility on him to be the leader, the way a husband most feels love is when his wife communicates willingness to follow his leadership and communicates her respect for him as a person.

Wives sometimes struggle with this. To them, respect is something you earn by proving yourself, but love is something you deserve by being a human. We speak often of the importance of "unconditional love," but we don't speak as often about the importance of respect. Actually, both love *and* respect are due to every person because they are made in the image of God. A wife is not expected to respect her husband for something he is not. You don't have to lie to yourself or your husband, pretending he has arrived in areas he hasn't. But don't let that stop you from respecting him for who he *is*—in particular, your husband.

Colossians 3:18 underscores this when it says, "Wives, submit yourselves unto your own husbands, *as it is fit in the Lord.*" The Bible does not teach that all women are supposed to submit to all men. But it does teach that a wife is to voluntarily place herself under the leadership of her husband and that this is pleasing to the Lord. As a man, I can tell you as well, that this is also incredibly motivating to a husband. What repeated requests cannot do, often a simple affirmation of respect *can* do.

Early in our marriage, my (Terrie) mother-in-law, knowing that I liked tennis, shared an illustration with me that has been a help to me: Imagine marriage as a tennis court with one side of the net being the role of the husband and the other being the role of the wife. As the wife, I know how I want my husband to fulfill his role. I know how I want him to serve, where on the court I want the ball to fall, how fast or slow I'd like it to come, and every other nuance of preference in how I want him to relate to me. I'm basically an expert at how he should play his game.

But if I am constantly over on his side of the court "teaching" him how to serve the ball to me, when he does it, I won't be on my side to return it to him. The ball will be in my court, and I will not.

This simple illustration has, through the years, helped me to focus on working my side of the net rather than my husband's. Even if he faults on the serve or the ball falls in a hard-to-reach spot on the court, I am far more likely to be able to keep the game going if I am ready to do my part than if I am teaching my husband how to do his part.

THE CURRENCY OF LOVE
(What a Wife Most Needs and Understands)

> *Husbands, love your wives, even as Christ also loved the church, and gave himself for it; That he might sanctify and cleanse it with the washing of water by the word, That he might present it to himself a glorious church, not having spot, or wrinkle, or any such thing; but that it should be holy and without blemish. So ought men to love their wives as their own bodies. He that loveth his wife loveth himself. For no man ever yet hated his own flesh; but nourisheth and cherisheth it, even as the Lord the church:*—EPHESIANS 5:25–29

We as men, in particular, often think that physical provision is what makes a marriage—putting food on the table, a car in the garage, fixing the washing machine, etc. Our goals tend to revolve around the material. While the role of provider is important, our wives need more than physical provision. They need frequent expressions of affection and love.

We have such flawed images of love that the kind of love God commands husbands to give to their wives is almost beyond our comprehension. So God gives us two specific ways husbands are to show love. First, love by sacrificing. This is what Christ did for the church—He gave *Himself* for it. The second way flows out of the first: love by serving.

Some years ago, I heard Dr. Daniel Kim, who has pastored the Bible Baptist Church in Seoul, Korea, for over fifty years, share the story of when he asked his prospective father-in-law for his daughter, Young Soon's, hand in marriage.

Before answering Dr. Kim, his father-in-law-to-be (also with the last name of Kim), told him a story from almost twenty years earlier. During the Korean War, he and his family were fleeing what is now North Korea for the south. It was a journey of many miles, made completely on foot and mostly under cover of darkness. Young Soon, now Dr. Kim's wife, was very young and would often cry—a great danger to herself and the entire group. In fact, the group they were with insisted that Mr. Kim separate from them for their safety. He continued on without them, carrying Young Soon the entire journey to the south.

As Mr. Kim finished his story, he looked at the young man asking for his daughter's hand in marriage. "I risked my life for her," he said, "and she is my most treasured possession. You may marry her if you promise to love her *like this*."

Most of us know nothing of that kind of sacrificial love for our wives. So God made it even more accessible for us to understand. Not only does God command me to love Terrie as Christ loved the church, but He commands me to love her as I love myself.

The ego of men is legendary; we think so highly of ourselves. So God tells us, "You know how to love yourself; love your wife like you love you, and you'll be doing well."

MAKING CONVERSIONS

If learning the currency exchange rate is a challenge in international travel, it is also a necessity. But the sooner you understand it and learn to automatically use it, the more you will enjoy your trip.

This is true of marriage as well. In many ways, marriage is a lifelong journey of exchanging currencies of love and respect. It is me purposefully learning to convert the respect I feel for Terrie into loving words and actions. And it is her learning to convert the love she feels for me into honoring words and actions.

How this is practically expressed will look different in every marriage. But below are five starter applications for you both:

5 Ways a Wife Can Communicate Respect to Her Husband (Terrie)

1. **Give genuine acceptance.** And by that, I mean, refuse to try to change your husband. Respect how God made him—his physical characteristics, personality, and even quirks. When you were dating, there were aspects of your husband's personality that attracted you to him. But after marriage, wives often discover a flip side of that characteristic that can drive them batty. (For example, the strong, silent, decisiveness you first admired may come with a reluctance to talk through decisions in depth.) The temptation is to mold your husband into someone who he is not and to forget that your husband is a person, not a set of features. This is neither respectful nor fair to him. Choose instead to give him full acceptance, and look for ways to communicate appreciation for specific aspects of his personality you admire.

2. **Support his decisions.** When we were in college, my husband was working a swing-shift job while taking a full load of classes and caring for a family. So when another student who was getting ready to graduate offered to sell him his window washing business with the promise that he was making thousands of dollars a week doing it, the offer was alluring.

I didn't feel so sure about it, however. For one thing, we knew nothing about running a business. But more importantly, we had zero extra money; in fact, we were barely getting by. The guy selling it said he'd give us a "real bargain"—$500 for his stack of 3x5 cards with all his customer information on them. This included no supplies and no guarantees. I didn't like it and told my husband that we shouldn't take the money we needed to pay basic bills to buy an unproven business.

The idea of relief from the swing shift won out, however, and he purchased the business. He began contacting every one of those "customers," only to find out that not a single one was interested. One of them even said, "Let me watch you do it once to decide." My husband washed his windows for free, only to find out that the guy just wanted a free window wash. In the end, the $500 was wasted. And $500 just then felt more like $5,000.

Throughout this entire business venture, I did my best to state my concerns and then support my husband's decision. Looking back, I wouldn't change it at all. Yes, we lost the money. Yes, I could have said, "I told you so. See if I ever trust you to make decisions again." But the truth is, we both learned, and because I determined to support him, we both ended up on the same team. We were broke, but we were broke together.

3. **Be his recreational partner.** Do you remember when you thought it was fun to watch football with your husband just so you could be together? Men are usually more event- or action-oriented, while women tend to be more conversation-oriented. While a deep conversation may be what makes you feel that he loves you, choosing to spend time with him doing something he enjoys makes him feel validated and loved.

4. **Pray for your husband's success.** Years ago, I determined that my prayers for my husband would be for his success, not for his changing. There may be a time when he has a blind spot in his life that I ask the Lord to reveal to him. But for the most part, I pray for God to bless him. If I spend my time in prayer for my husband, thinking about how he needs to improve, I will leave my place of prayer with a stronger desire to change him than to support him. Conversely, if I spend my time thanking God for his strengths and praying for his successes, I leave prayer with a heart to be part of those answers.

5. **Praise him—privately and publicly.** Men are so cut down by society today that a wife who verbalizes praise is incredibly attractive to a man. A simple note left in his sock drawer—"Honey, thank you for being such a hard worker. I admire you for it."—is like a windfall

of respect currency to a man. Tell him in private moments together how much you love to be with him. And then talk about him positively to others—your children, your friends, on social media, etc.—when he is present. Public praise is a magnifier, multiplying its effect by the number of people hearing it. The flip side of this is to never, *never* belittle your husband to others. If you have a concern, talk with him about it. But loose comments in front of him or talking negatively about him behind his back will deeply hurt him and ultimately hurt your relationship.

5 Ways a Husband Can Communicate Love to His Wife (Paul)

1. **Seek to understand her.** First Peter 3:7 says, "Likewise, ye husbands, dwell with them *according to knowledge....*" Get to know your wife. Study what her needs are, as well as her likes, dislikes, and preferences. Whether it be a Diet Coke or a special place she likes to celebrate your anniversary, you honor her by caring enough to learn and remember.

2. **Take initiative in spiritual matters.** A husband's leadership in the home isn't just about financial decisions; it is to be spiritual leadership as well. Ephesians 5:26 says, "That he might sanctify and

cleanse it with the washing of water by the word."
While this verse is primarily referring to how Christ
leads the church, it is making the correlation that the
husband is to do the same. Even if your personality
isn't that of a "born leader," you can be proactive in
initiating spiritual growth as a couple or family. This
may start simply by beginning a time of prayer and
Scripture reading together before bed. It certainly
includes praying for and with your wife and taking
your family to church. It could also include initiating
discussions with your wife about spiritual matters
and sharing with her aspects of what God is doing in
your life.

3. **Give and communicate security.** Whether or not
    you and your wife both work, you must assume the
    leadership and responsibility of providing for your
    family's needs. First Timothy 5:8 says, "But if any
    provide not for his own, and specially for those of
    his own house, he hath denied the faith, and is worse
    than an infidel." Being a responsible provider gives
    your wife security. But your wife also needs you to
    give emotional and spiritual security. She needs you
    to communicate your love often, tenderly, and freely.
    This is done by nonsexual caresses, verbal affirmations
    of love, and frequent moments of thoughtfulness.

4. **Spend time together as a family.** It doesn't have to be Disneyland. A day at the park, an evening playing games, or even an hour of you playing with the kids means the world to your wife. Women are wired to care for family relationships in a deep way that often holds families together. You communicate love to her when you spend time together as a family.

5. **Communicate appreciation for who she is.** Even when it comes to communicating appreciation for what she *does,* we men tend to fall short. But your wife wants to know you love her regardless of what she does for you. When was the last time you told her, "Sweetheart, I just want you to know that no matter what happens, I'm always going to be grateful that you let me be your husband. Thank you for being the amazing person you are"?

SPEND iT!

We have spent most of this chapter describing the challenge of remembering to exchange the heart currency you feel with the heart currency your spouse needs and best understands.

The thing about currency, however, is that regardless of what form it is—pesos, dollars, pounds, yuan, or even

Monopoly money—it doesn't buy anything unless you use it. It doesn't matter what country you are in or what the exchange rate is or how well you understand the exchange rate. If the money stays in your pocket, you get no value from it.

As we close this chapter, I want to encourage you to *spend* your currency on your spouse. Don't just *think* love or respect. Don't just consider the ways you want your spouse to show you love or respect. Don't be so concerned about not knowing how to make conversions that you keep it in your pocket.

Go ahead and spend it. Giving love and respect to your spouse is the best way to invest in your marriage.

By the grave of
Charles Spurgeon

(left) In front of Windsor
Palace in London

(right) Shopping on Oxford
Street in London

(left) Meeting a lion
cub in Cabo San Lucas

(right) A productive
day in the woods

FOUR

IT'S A TWO-LANE HIGHWAY

Communication

One of the frequent road trips we took in the early years of our marriage was the six hour drive from our home in San Dimas, California, to Terrie's parents' home in San Jose.

I was in Bible college at the time and keeping a whirlwind schedule. I had classes from 7:30 AM–12:30 PM, ran home for a quick sandwich and a moment to change, and then worked until midnight. I'd come home and study for the next day's class, catch a few hours of sleep, and then do it again the next day. Needless to say, I was always exhausted.

On one now-memorable trip up to San Jose, we were supposed to arrive at Terrie's parents' by late morning for a birthday party. We left San Dimas at 1:00 AM, just after I had come home from work. I was still alert, so I drove while Terrie slept.

The freeways in heavily-populated Southern California typically have concrete medians between the northbound and southbound traffic, but Interstate 5 further north has large stretches with no raised median— just a space of ground between the two directions of traffic. This became a significant fact halfway through our drive that night.

Terrie woke up when she felt the car bouncing in unfamiliar fashion and then heard tires on rumble strips. She sat up to see that we had just driven through the median and, still driving north, were entering the south-bound lanes of I-5. At full speed. (I'm such a good driver that I can drive in my sleep.)

Obviously, we lived. And thankfully, we didn't wreck. But that was only by the grace of God and Terrie's quick response to wake me up.

Our memorable road trip parallels the communication of many marriages. Without some quick intervention, there is going to be a tragic wreck with terrible carnage.

The words we speak hold tremendous power. And their power is increased exponentially when we speak them to people we love. If a stranger walked up to you in the grocery store, and said, "I hate you," you'd probably wonder what was wrong with him, and move on. But if your spouse said, "I hate you," you'd be devastated.

Our words also hold lasting power long after we speak them. You can probably remember within a matter of seconds the most hurtful thing someone you love said to you. Conversely, you can probably also remember unexpected words of praise or thanks from someone you loved or respected. Although these words may have only lasted mere seconds, they had a powerful influence on you

This is true in marriage as well. The words you say to one another have extreme significance. Proverbs 18:21 tells us, "Death and life are in the power of the tongue: and they that love it shall eat the fruit thereof."

Too often, Christian homes are no different than non-Christian homes in communication. Couples who wouldn't think of physically abusing one another may hurt the other even more deeply with sarcastic or cutting words. Husbands demean their wives, and wives belittle their husbands. There's yelling and screaming or silence and cutting off. But no one wins in this kind of environment— not the spouse who hurts the other and not the spouse who clams up and refuses to speak.

Perhaps the saddest aspect of communication dysfunctions is not the harm that is happening, but the good that is being missed. God created us with a *need* for relational connection, and marriage is the pinnacle of fulfilling that need. But it requires that we communicate with one another in godly, positive, and kind ways. It requires that we purposefully drive both directions on the communication highway—listening and speaking into one another's hearts.

A relationship with poor communication is like a traffic jam. You're not going anywhere, or at least not very fast. But grace-filled communication opens one another's hearts and allows you to travel further together. Ephesians 4 teaches us how to have this kind of healthy, godly communication:

> *Wherefore putting away lying, speak every man truth with his neighbour: for we are members one of another. Be ye angry, and sin not: let not the sun go down upon your wrath: Neither give place to the devil. Let him that stole steal no more: but rather let him labour, working with his hands the thing which is good, that he may have to give to him that needeth. Let no corrupt communication proceed out of your mouth, but that which is good to the use of edifying, that it may minister grace unto the hearers. And grieve not the holy*

Spirit of God, whereby ye are sealed unto the day of redemption. Let all bitterness, and wrath, and anger, and clamour, and evil speaking, be put away from you, with all malice: And be ye kind one to another, tenderhearted, forgiving one another, even as God for Christ's sake hath forgiven you.
—EPHESIANS 4:25–32

In this chapter, let's look at four guardrails providing safety and access along the highway of marriage communication.

THE GUARDRAIL OF TRUTH

Wherefore putting away lying, speak every man truth with his neighbour: for we are members one of another.—EPHESIANS 4:25

This guardrail lines either side of the communication highway, protecting travelers from two ditches. On one side, there is the ditch of speaking anything less than the truth, and on the other side is the ditch of not speaking at all.

No secrets

Lying has become a way of life for too many Christians. From hiding the truth, to exaggerating the facts, to bold-faced lies, any breach in truthfulness will damage a marriage because it destroys the trust needed for real communication to take place.

Marriage is not a place for secrets. This means no hidden websites. No private texts or secret social media. No hidden checking accounts or credit cards. No blocking access to current accounts. No secret stashes of porn. No hidden relationships. Every part of either of your lives should be fully open to the other.

Sin thrives in the shadows. When you hide part of your life from your spouse, no matter how innocent or noble the reason seems, you open your life and your marriage to disaster. Jesus unequivocally stated that the devil is the father of lies and that there is "no truth in him" (John 8:44). Any departure from truth in a Christian's life opens the door to the devil.

Where there have been secrets in the past, they must be brought out into the open, repented of, and sought forgiveness for. This can be painful, and you may need to seek the help of your pastor or a godly counselor. But don't go on living in the shadows. That hidden place in your life will pull your marriage into the ditch.

One of the greatest lies Satan uses to keep secrets hidden is that if you exposed the truth of hidden sin in your life to your spouse, it would put a worse strain on your marriage. This is true if you are thinking to expose that sin with the expectation that you will be allowed to go on participating in it. But it is not true where you expose it before it is found out and are humble, repentant, and willing to take whatever steps are necessary to bring victory in your life and healing in your marriage. Proverbs 28:13 is both a warning against hiding sin and an encouragement to those who want freedom: "He that covereth his sins shall not prosper: but whoso confesseth and forsaketh them shall have mercy."

I remember a couple who came for counseling some years ago. Unbeknownst to me, the husband had previously lived a double life including an affair, and, also unbeknownst to me, he wanted to tell his wife in my presence. As this husband began telling his wife about his unfaithfulness, she was first shocked and then enraged. I remember her running out of my office in hysterics and my secretary running after her. Long story (including many hours of counseling) short, this husband demonstrated genuine repentance before God and to his wife, and she received God's grace to forgive her husband. Today, their marriage is strong and growing. Had he kept his sin against her a secret, I doubt their marriage would still be intact. I know that it would not be strong. You just can't build a strong marriage on dishonesty or untruthfulness. Truth is always the best foundation for a relationship.

Maybe you have no "big secrets" your spouse doesn't know. But is everything about your communication fully open and transparent? If your spouse knew everything you know, would he or she think you had been less than honest?

One of the best ways to promote transparency in marriage is to embrace accountability with one another. Some people feel threatened by accountability. They think it implies a lack of trust. Actually the opposite is true. When you *choose* accountability, you *build* trust.

As we were preparing this book for publication, Vice President Mike Pence made the news because of an article that mentioned, "Mike Pence…never eats alone with a woman other than his wife."[1] The media *ridiculed* the Pences for this. In reality, their decision was wise. In a political world where scandals of infidelity are rampant, why would it be thought of as anything less than honorable for a couple to set boundaries of protection around their marriage? Terrie and I have boundaries as well. One of those is that as a pastor, I will not counsel a lady alone behind a closed door. Another is that we give each other immediate and unrestricted access at all times. Terrie can walk into my office at any time regardless of what meeting I may be in or who else may be present. When she calls, I answer my phone, and vice versa.

I often tell couples, "Elevate accountability; eliminate doubt." If you're going to be home late from work, don't leave your spouse wondering where you are or who you're with. Make a quick phone call to explain why you're late and when you'll be home. Your spouse has the right to know where you are, what you are doing, who you are talking with, everything that is on your phone and in your emails, and any other part of your life. So don't feel interrogated or violated because your husband or wife asks, and don't accuse your spouse of mistrusting you. Eliminate any doubt in the other's mind by elevating accountability between the two of you.

Safe sharing

There is more to truthfulness than what you *don't* say; there is also what you *do* say. Ephesians 4:25 not only warns us not to lie, but it also instructs us to speak truth. Good communication is proactive communication where your spouse is the one person on earth with whom you can and do share anything and everything.

Regular communication is the highway to complete openness. Without the real exchange of thoughts and emotions, there will be no depth to your relationship.

Men sometimes feel anxious about too much emphasis on communication. Often men are reluctant to share deeply and transparently, and many don't think they need to. They don't always find it easy to share their thoughts and feelings, or, for that matter, to know what to do with someone else's thoughts and feelings. But without learning healthy, godly communication, your relationship is going nowhere fast.

Men, please understand that your wife *needs* to talk. Even as sexual intimacy is a need for you, so real communication is a need for your wife. In fact, the more you willingly engage in heart-level communication with her, the safer she will feel and thus the more responsive she will be to you physically.

It took me some time before I understood that Terrie's desire to talk when I come home in the evening is not selfish, but it is a real need in her life. I'm not always in a frame of mind to talk immediately when I walk in the door. But since she knows that I am committed to hearing about her day and want to hear everything else she has to share, it's no longer a problem if I suggest we talk later in the evening. As I have grown in this area, it has so enhanced our relationship. And over the years, I've grown to truly enjoy these times and have learned to share my thoughts and heart equally with her.

In the process, I've learned something else about Terrie. She needs a safe environment if she is to share freely. She needs to know that I am genuinely listening and that I won't scorn or belittle her ideas. For her to "speak truth" with me, she needs to know it's safe.

A safe environment for communication usually means something different to a man than it does to a woman. To most women, a safe environment is knowing that her husband is listening and that her feelings will not be ridiculed or made light of. To most men, however, a safe environment is knowing that what he shares will not go further than that conversation. That is, it will not be shared with her mother, her friends, or anyone else. A wife who learns to keep confidence with what her husband shares with her will find her husband more willing to share.

This difference is significant because women tend to be more open with their feelings. For Terrie to share with someone else what a mutual friend shared with her may very well not be thought of as a breach in trust for any of them. But if Terrie shared with a mutual friend what *I* share with her, it feels different to me. A man's emotions may be simpler or more straightforward than a woman's (and they often are), but he is generally less willing to expose them. A wife who understands this can be the virtuous woman Proverbs 31:11 speaks of when it says, "The heart of her husband doth safely trust in her...."

The kind of environment needed for both spouses to feel safe communicating is summed up in Ephesians 4:15: "But speaking the truth in love...." There are two sides to speaking the truth—speaking it, and speaking it in love.

Without the guardrail of truth, marriage communication winds up in a ditch fast.

THE GUARDRAIL OF INDIGNATION

> *Be ye angry, and sin not: let not the sun go down upon your wrath: Neither give place to the devil.*—EPHESIANS 4:26–27

What about when communication (or the lack of it) leads to an impasse in going forward together? No real relationships avoid conflict. Any relationship that does either has no depth or has underlying stress that one or the other will not acknowledge.

When you face a point of conflict that evokes anger, determine to stand together in your anger. That is, be angry together at the problem, not at each other. Henry Ford said, "Don't find a fault; find a remedy." You are on the same team. Rather than pointing fingers at one another, jointly tackle the problem that is hurting or threatening your relationship.

Determine also that you will never go to bed angry with one another. Ever.

This doesn't mean that you will always be able to develop an answer to problems before sleep. There have been a few times when Terrie or I had to simply reach for the other's hand, reaffirm our commitment to solving the problem, and suggest giving it to the Lord until the morning. Even in those rare instances, praying together and committing to stand together against the problem diffuses the anger and draws our hearts closer to one another. As we'll see more fully in chapter 6, it also helps protect our hearts from Satan's advances against our relationship.

The guardrail of proactive indignation helps you protect the most important part of your life—your heart. This is why Proverbs 4:23 instructs, "Keep thy heart with all diligence; for out of it are the issues of life." Guard your heart, and you will guard your marriage.

Refusing to direct your anger toward your spouse gives you another advantage in communication—the ability to *listen*. James 1:19 says, "Wherefore my beloved brethren, let every man be swift to hear, slow to speak, slow to wrath." Your grandmother probably said it differently: "There is a reason you have two ears and only one mouth."

Sometimes we *hear* our spouse without actually *listening* to him or her. When Terrie and I first moved to Lancaster, we lived in a duplex near the train station. All night long, we'd hear the trains coming and going. It would start with a whistle far in the distance. Soon, we'd hear the rumble of the train coming closer. Then another whistle. Then the train would whiz by. Another whistle as it neared the station…. We'd lie in bed at night listening to the trains and wishing we could sleep.

By the time we moved out of that duplex several months later, however, we didn't even notice the trains. They still rumbled past several times a day and through the night, but we had been able to tune them out. We *heard* them, but we were no longer *listening*.

When our reflex response to a situation is anger, we miss hearing the heart of our spouse. But when we guard our own heart against anger, we are free to really listen heart to heart and ultimately find a solution together.

THE GUARDRAIL OF KINDNESS

Let no corrupt communication proceed out of your mouth...—EPHESIANS 4:29

Have you ever stepped back and listened to yourself and thought, "Wow! I sound harsh"? I have. I suppose all of us have. Amazingly, the basic courtesies we show strangers are sometimes absent in our dearest relationships, particularly marriage.

If you want to have kind speech, it helps to set parameters—like the out-of-bounds areas in a basketball game. Having limits protects you from saying things in the heat of the moment that you'll regret later. The four simple rules for communication that I will suggest here are so basic you might be tempted to overlook them. But unless you have already adopted these rules in your home, I'd ask you to consider committing to them.

1. **Never threaten with divorce.** Usually whoever mentions divorce first does it to try to get the other's attention. But once you crack that door open, even suggesting divorce as a possibility, you are giving Satan entrance to push it open wider. Terrie and I made a commitment before we were even married that the "d-word" would never enter our disagreements or be hinted at as a possibility. If you've already crossed that line, why not pray together, renewing your commitment to your marriage and making today a fresh start from which *divorce* is never mentioned again?

2. **Never argue in front of the kids.** The greatest gift you can give your children is to love your spouse. Sometimes parents purposefully involve their children in arguments or disagreements in order to shame the other spouse or get the children to take sides. Sometimes parents are just self-focused enough to not consider the impact their fighting has on their children. But hearing their parents fight *does* influence children. It makes them insecure, worries them that the disagreement is their fault, and even impacts their academics because of the emotional

distraction it creates. Make it a rule: you will stand united in love in the presence of your children and will work out disagreements privately.

3. **Never attack personally.** This is the practical outworking of attacking a problem rather than a person. Instead of accusing, "You always leave your socks on the bathroom floor because you don't care how much work I do around here," explain your vantage point and ask a question: "I'm feeling overwhelmed with keeping the bathroom clean. I know it seems like a small thing, but would you mind putting your socks in the hamper in the bedroom after your shower?" Don't presume to know your spouse's motives or turn an action into a lack of character.

4. **Take breaks during tense moments.** When you sense frustration or anger rising, take a few minutes to collect your emotions and to remember that you *love* your spouse before reengaging in conversation. Proverbs 29:11 warns, "A fool uttereth all his mind: but a wise man keepeth it in till afterwards." Instead of giving your spouse a piece of your mind, choose to give yourself a slice of time. Terrie and I have learned that if we will take a few minutes (and be willing to give them to the other when he or she needs them), we are far less likely to say something we will regret. It's

kind of like a car overheating on a road trip. The fact that it is overheating means there is a problem, but it's best to let the engine cool before addressing it.

We experienced what it was like to deal with a consistently-overheating engine early in our marriage. I was still in Bible college, and we had just had our first baby, Danielle. Needing a reliable car with more room than my little pickup truck, we were excited to buy an orange 1978 Honda five-speed hatchback wagon from a Christian man who assured us that he had just recently refurbished the engine and that everything was in tip-top shape. We were, at that time, driving 150 miles each weekend to the Coachella Valley where we were planting a church. The temperatures were routinely 105–110 degrees.

On the way down the first weekend in our new wagon, the air conditioning went out. And on the way back to Los Angeles, the engine overheated. For the next several weeks, until we could afford to replace the radiator, we had to carry water with us and plan extra travel time for multiple stops to let the overheated engine cool, open the radiator cap, and pour water in.

Although it is best to not let your car overheat in the first place (just as it is best to not let disagreements in your marriage become heated), when it happens, you need to let the engine cool before pouring water in. Even so, it's wise when you are frustrated to give each other some space before attempting to resolve the disagreement.

There is one caveat to the practice of taking a time out, however: neither spouse should use it as a way to shut down conversation. If you need to take time out, it is your responsibility to suggest another time to reopen the discussion later.

You've heard the schoolyard rhyme: "Sticks and stones may break my bones, but words will never hurt me." It's not true. Words *do* hurt. If you have been using your words to tear one another down, determine today to instead use your words to build one another up. That leads us to our final guardrail.

THE GUARDRAIL OF EDIFICATION

...but that which is good to the use of edifying, that it may minister grace unto the hearers.—EPHESIANS 4:29

We began this chapter noting the power of our words. For all the power they have to wound and hurt one another, they also have tremendous power to build. In fact, to *edify* means "to build." (Think of the word *edifice*—a building.) And if there is one action that love does, it is build others. First Corinthians 8:1 tells us, "...charity edifieth"—it builds.

Every time we use our words to criticize, we are saying to our spouse, "I don't love you." But every time we speak words of encouragement and praise, we are communicating love in one of the most meaningful ways possible.

Encouraging words are so powerful that Ephesians 4:29 says they "minister grace unto the hearers." You can, through the very words you speak, be a dispenser of grace to your spouse.

In Terrie's book, *The Choice Is Yours,* she provides a list from Scripture of the positive influence our words can have.[2] As you read through this list, consider how you can bring this kind of communication into your marriage as you build your spouse with the kinds of words described in these verses.

Positive words give instruction and wisdom.

The mouth of the just bringeth forth wisdom: but the froward tongue shall be cut out.—PROVERBS 10:31

The tongue of the wise useth knowledge aright: but the mouth of fools poureth out foolishness.—PROVERBS 15:2

The heart of the wise teacheth his mouth, and addeth learning to his lips.—PROVERBS 16:23

Positive words give direction.

Hear counsel, and receive instruction, that thou mayest be wise in thy latter end.
—PROVERBS 19:20

Ointment and perfume rejoice the heart: so doth the sweetness of a man's friend by hearty counsel.—PROVERBS 27:9

Positive words praise the Lord.

I will bless the LORD at all times: his praise shall continually be in my mouth.
—PSALM 34:1

O Lord, open thou my lips; and my mouth shall shew forth thy praise.—PSALM 51:15

Positive words encourage others.

A word fitly spoken is like apples of gold in pictures of silver.—PROVERBS 25:11

A man hath joy by the answer of his mouth: and a word spoken in due season, how good is it!—PROVERBS 15:23

The Lord GOD hath given me the tongue of the learned, that I should know how to speak a word in season to him that is weary...
—ISAIAH 50:4

Positive words are pleasant and appropriate.

The lips of the righteous know what is acceptable: but the mouth of the wicked speaketh frowardness.—PROVERBS 10:32

The thoughts of the wicked are an abomination to the Lord: but the words of the pure are pleasant words.—PROVERBS 15:26

Pleasant words are as an honeycomb, sweet to the soul, and health to the bones.
—PROVERBS 16:24

She openeth her mouth with wisdom; and in her tongue is the law of kindness.
—PROVERBS 31:26

Positive words facilitate healing.

The mouth of a righteous man is a well of life: but violence covereth the mouth of the wicked.—PROVERBS 10:11

A wholesome tongue is a tree of life: but perverseness therein is a breach in the spirit.—PROVERBS 15:4

There is that speaketh like the piercings of a sword: but the tongue of the wise is health.
—PROVERBS 12:18

Positive words bring security and truth.

Have not I written to thee excellent things in counsels and knowledge, That I might make thee know the certainty of the words of truth; that thou mightest answer the words of truth to them that send unto thee?—PROVERBS 22:20–21

You have the power, like no one else in the world, to build up and encourage your spouse. Use this power.

KEEP DRIVING

When Terrie woke me up that day as we were traveling north on the southbound lanes of Interstate 5, I was shocked at what had happened, and I knew I had to think quickly.

I could have slammed on the brake and just sat there, worried that I would do something wrong. Had I done that, someone else surely would have crashed into us.

I also could have pulled to the nearest shoulder of the road, and waited for a tow truck to bring us to the other side. Had I done that, we wouldn't have made progress in our journey.

Instead, I hit the gas and quickly turned the wheel right. We re-crossed the median—this time on purpose—and continued our journey. (I was fully awake now!)

As you work at communication in marriage, you will have times when you mess up. You'll scrape the guardrails we looked at in this chapter. Sometimes you'll swerve into the ditch. You may end up traveling in the exact opposite direction you intended to go. But even when you struggle to go forward or when you mess up by overcorrecting, don't just put your communication in park and quit trying. Don't shut down or leave all the communicating to your spouse.

Communication is a two-lane highway, and it works best if you keep moving on it. There may be some frustrations along the way, but it is the highway to happiness in your relationship. So keep driving.

(top) Overlooking one of the
oldest golf courses in the world
in Saint Andrews, Scotland

(bottom) On the front steps
of the church in the Coachella
Valley, just before getting back
in the car for a long, hot ride.

FiVE
ROADBLOCKS
Conflict

On our most recent trip to Israel, we had the opportunity to visit Abraham's tomb in Hebron, seventeen miles south of Jerusalem. If you are familiar with Israel's geography and current news, you know that this is the region known as the West Bank and is a constant hotbed of unrest.

As we approached Hebron, we came up on a sign posted by the Israeli government that read (in Hebrew, Arabic, and English), "The entrance for Israeli citizens is forbidden, dangerous to your lives, and is against the Israeli law." Suddenly, I began wondering, *Why are we going here? Is it worth it?* We proceeded, and came to our first roadblock where Israeli soldiers checked our bus to be sure there were no Israeli citizens.

As we drove a little further, we came to another roadblock, this one manned by Palestinian soldiers. The soldiers filled our bus, demanded all of our passports, and succeeded in making us feel incredibly uncomfortable as they questioned us. Finally, they returned our passports and motioned us on.

When we finally entered Hebron, there were two police stations—one Palestinian and one Israeli—with soldiers and police by the hundreds, all carrying machine guns.

Although this experience was tense for us Americans, in reality, roadblocks in the Holy Land are common. In fact, they are much like conflicts in marriage—they are part of life, and they have the potential to either escalate into full-blown combat or diffuse into nothing more than a delay.

The difference between the two, however, is that while physical roadblocks are out in the open, most relational conflict happens in relative privacy. You may look at couples with "the perfect marriage" and assume that great marriages never have conflict. The truth is, conflict, or at least disagreement, is fairly common in marriage. The difference between a strong marriage and a weak marriage is how partners handle that conflict.

I (Terrie) grew up in a home with an alcoholic father, and have always been sensitive to conflict, especially early in our marriage. To me, a raised voice was a short warning before verbal and/or physical abuse. For years, I had developed coping mechanisms of emotional sensitivity and withdrawal: the moment I sensed tension beginning to build in any relationship (and I was good at sensing it), my reflex was to withdraw. This became a difficulty in marriage because the best way past a roadblock is through it, but I was stopping short.

Making the situation even more complex was my expectation that Christian couples never fight. Coming from an unsaved home, I was so looking forward to building a truly Christian home with my husband and was determined that our marriage would be Christ honoring in every way—including no disagreement. To be sure, I knew in my head that every marriage is comprised of two imperfect people, but I still had a heart expectation that was far more idealistic than reality.

For these reasons, the first fight we had that included raised voices was devastating to me. I remember how, as we went our separate ways, my stomach tied up in knots as I realized with horror that our marriage was probably on the verge of total collapse. Wanting to fight for what was left of our marriage, I turned back to my husband and suggested we get counseling.

I was surprised at how shocked he looked. And I was even more surprised when he simply said, "Sweetheart, I'm so sorry for raising my voice. I love you and wish I hadn't said that the way I did." And then he proceeded to suggest ways we could solve our difference of opinion.

I went from devastation to shock. I had no idea that conflict could be solved so simply. We easily made up, and now neither of us can even remember what that incident was about. Over the years, we have learned together that what makes a Christian marriage distinct is not that conflict never happens. (It is impossible for two people to so completely share their lives with one another for a period of years and *not* face points of disagreement.) The difference is in how Christians respond to conflict. If you learn to respond in a godly, thoughtful, and resolution-orientated way, the very process of working through it together will build your confidence in one another and strengthen your marriage. If, however, you respond in a reactionary, dismissive, or unkind way, each conflict will breed underlying anger and resentment between you both, which will undermine your marriage.

In our previous chapter, we looked at principles for Christian communication. In this chapter, we'll see the application of those principles in relation to conflict.[1]

person's point of view. Rather than apologizing, we defend our behavior. Where there is contention in a relationship, pride is at work.

Pettiness—Some things really are too small to argue about. Pathological pettiness turns every disagreement into right versus wrong, with one person having to be proven right. This is usually rooted in selfishness and pride.

Fear and insecurity—When someone who has been hurt feels a conflict coming on, often they withdraw to avoid it, rather than engaging in resolution. Unfortunately, problems left unsolved or with only surface solutions usually fester. The increasing tension from what could have been solved grows larger, which, in turn, makes an insecure or fearful person even less likely to be willing to deal with it.

First John 4:18 provides the answer to fear: "There is no fear in love; but perfect love casteth out fear: because fear hath torment. He that feareth is not made perfect in love." Where fear is involved, couples need to identify that fear before solving a conflict and assure the other that in whatever way the conflict is solved, their non-negotiable is their love for one another. This was significant for Terrie and me. As she mentioned at the beginning of this chapter, she had great fear of conflict itself. It was some time before I learned to recognize her fear and we both understood the source of it. Recognizing it helped me understand that a

WHY CONFLICT ARISES

Our first fight was at our wedding reception. More accurately, it was in the car immediately after the reception—but it started at the reception.

For months prior to our wedding, Terrie had invested untold hours into making reception favors—fabric roses with a candied almond as the center—for our special day. She explained to me ahead of time that during the reception she and I were to take a basket of these around and personally thank each person who was there, giving them a rose as we did so. To Terrie, this labor of love was a way to express personal gratitude to those who had invested in our lives. I viewed it as a thoughtful idea and didn't think much more of it…until the reception.

After we had delivered roses to about six people, I realized this was going to take way too long. Totally forgetting the reasons Terrie had made the roses and why she wanted to hand deliver each of them, I saw that basket only as an obstacle to getting out of the reception and on to our honeymoon. Inspired with a great idea, I grabbed the mic from our emcee and announced, "If there is anyone who would like one of these roses, come up and get one!"

My idea was a success. We were immediately flocked by every child in the room, and I watched with joy as the roses disappeared. I, the rose-conquering-hero, whisked Terrie out to the car, and we were off.

We were hardly away from the church when I looked over and saw Terrie's lip quivering and her eyes filling with tears. I couldn't believe it! How in the world could she be unhappy? We were just starting the happiest week of our lives!

"What's wrong, honey?"

Through broken sobs she got out, "How could you give out all the roses…to the kids? I didn't even get to thank those ladies who came to our wedding…who mentored me…who invested in our lives…they came to our wedding, and we just ignored them…."

So there it was—we had been married less than an hour, and already we had conflict.

In that moment, Terrie and I both thought that our disagreement was over candied-almond roses. Looking back, that wasn't the issue at all. The conflict was actually over a difference of perspective and was rooted in insensitivity on my part. (When Terrie tells this story, she also says no one at the wedding cared and it was rooted in making a bigger deal out of something small on her part. But, remember, it's Terrie who says this—not me!)

So what *does* cause conflict in marriage? There are many surface causes, but we've boiled these down to several common root issues:

Selfishness—I'm not saying that every disagreement should be solved by one spouse continually yielding

or saying that what does matter to him or her doesn't matter. But often conflict is caused because we care more about ourselves than we do about the other person or the relationship—at least at that moment.

Selfishness is not the absence of love; it is *self-love*. James 4:1 gets to the heart of it: "From whence come wars and fightings among you? come they not hence, even of your lusts that war in your members?" It is our insistence on having what we want—even at the expense of the other person's happiness—that can create conflict.

Selfishness seems to have been the cause of conflict at the church in Philippi as Paul wrote, "I beseech Euodias, and beseech Syntyche, that they be of the same mind in the Lord" (Philippians 4:2). Two chapters earlier he wrote a verse we have already looked at, "Look not every man on his own things, but every man also on the things of others" (Philippians 2:4). For your marriage to be a Philippians 4:2 marriage, where you are "of the same mind in the Lord," you will both need to practice Philippians 2:4, caring more about the other than about yourself.

Pride—Proverbs 13:10 says, "Only by pride cometh contention: but with the well advised is wisdom." *Conflict* and *contention* do not have to be synonymous. It is possible to disagree without being contentious, but constant conflict usually includes contention. Pride makes us unwilling to admit when we are wrong or to acknowledge another

touch of anger on my part *felt* like a blast of anger to Terrie. It also helped Terrie understand to pause and remember that I was not her alcoholic father and freed her to de-escalate her perceptions.

Satanic Attack—There can be no doubt that marriage faces enemies that are designed and empowered by Satan himself. Because marriage is a picture of Christ and the church (Ephesians 5:32), Satan *hates* it and wants to destroy it. Every time a Christian family is broken, the testimony of Christ is harmed. Every time a couple lets conflict grow between them, their own walk with the Lord is harmed.

You have an enemy who is out to destroy your relationship. First Peter 5:8 warns, "Be sober, be vigilant; because your adversary the devil, as a roaring lion, walketh about, seeking whom he may devour." Recognizing this shouldn't make you afraid or "see a demon behind every bush" in conflict. But it should add urgency to dealing with conflict in a godly way rather than reacting in pride or selfishness or pretending no conflict exists.

One or more of these five causes is usually at the heart of ongoing conflict within marriage. Often they seem small (what's a little selfishness in an otherwise okay relationship?), but if these unhealthy roots are allowed to remain without being addressed, the relationship will weaken over time.

BUiLDiNG WALLS

One of our favorite places we've been to together is Ireland. In addition to its breathtaking beauty, Ireland, like the rest of Europe, is steeped in rich history and, of course, wars.

Much of the conflict in Ireland over the years has been over politically inspired Catholic versus Protestant disagreements. Northern Ireland (which is part of Great Britain), in particular, has been fraught with religious-based wars, the most recent of which is referred to as The Troubles—a series of conflicts that lasted over thirty years and ended with the Belfast Agreement of 1998.

During The Troubles, tempers were hot and conflict would easily spark across the city. The solution was what is now known as "peace walls" or "peace lines." Throughout Belfast, fences and walls spontaneously appeared to separate Catholic and Protestant neighborhoods. The peace lines that we saw there range in length from a few hundred yards to miles. They are made of iron, brick, and/or steel and are up to twenty-five feet high.

Their name is deceiving, however. Nothing about these walls created peace; they only kept a sort of truce because they separated angry people. That's not conflict *resolution;* it's conflict *avoidance.*

Ineffective responses to marriage conflict are like erecting a peace wall between you and your spouse. A wall may provide ceasefire, but it can't resolve the issue. The more of these walls you build, the more difficult it is to pursue relational intimacy.

So, what are the ineffective responses to conflict in marriage? Here are ten of the most common:

Failure to acknowledge the problem—Denial is dangerous to your relationship. When one spouse will not acknowledge that conflict exists, it damages the relationship and discourages the other spouse. First John 1:6 warns us concerning our relationship with the Lord, to not allow sin to go unaddressed, ignoring how it affects our fellowship with Him: "If we say that we have fellowship with him, and walk in darkness, we lie, and do not the truth."

This imagery of walking in darkness versus walking in the light can be applied to the marriage relationship as well. I've lost track of how many couples I've counseled who for a period of months or years had allowed serious conflict to continue while the whole time putting on their church face every Sunday morning and pretending all was well.

Withdrawal from real relationship development—Many couples come to the point where they decide intimacy and oneness are beyond reach. Perhaps for the sake of their children or their convictions about the permanence of marriage, they stay married. But they withdraw their spirit emotionally and spiritually, and often withdraw physically as well. They live in the same house, but they settle for less than God means for their marriage to be.

Spiritualizing the problem—Sometimes a spouse in counseling will say, "Well, the devil's just fighting us." Although that is true, spiritual talk about a problem isn't the same as rolling up your sleeves to deal with it. We do need to be alert to attacks from the devil, but we also need to take responsibility for resolving conflict.

Gunnysacking—It's amazing how well our memories can work when it comes to holding on to the past faults of our spouse. I've counseled couples who have said during their appointment, "But you wouldn't believe what he said on November 18, 1992." Harboring past hurts is like keeping them in an internal gunnysack to be able to dump out during disagreements later. No good can come from that. Once a matter has been addressed and forgiven, it should never come up again. This is the way God deals with our sins. "I, even I, am he that blotteth out thy transgressions for mine own sake, and will not remember thy sins" (Isaiah 43:25).

Attacking the person instead of the problem—You have a gift from God in the person of your spouse. Attacking the person you married devalues God's gift and undermines your relationship. When it comes to conflict, work together to seek out the causes rather than turning your arguments against your spouse.

Blaming your spouse—"I'm the way I am because of the stress she puts me under." "I wouldn't lose my temper if he didn't annoy me so much." This tactic goes back to the Garden of Eden. Adam blamed the first sin on Eve. She turned around and blamed the serpent (Genesis 3:9–13). It is part of our fallen nature to pass the buck. We instinctively try to avoid responsibility for our words and actions. But you cannot resolve conflict until you accept responsibility for your responses and resolve to be part of the solution.

Desiring to win at any cost—There are some arguments that are better lost. Nobody really wins in marital strife. You may think you have "won" a battle when you've really just robbed a piece of your spouse's heart. Always remember that your relationship is far more important than who wins any one particular argument.

Giving in to avoid conflict—On the opposite end of the spectrum is someone who "gives in," not in a humble, sacrificial way, but simply to make the conflict stop. Someone who consistently avoids disagreement by just saying, "Whatever you want," isn't contributing to building a relationship. If you are giving in in the spirit of 1 Peter 5:5—"…all of you be subject one to another, and be clothed with humility…"—that's godly. But if you are giving in as an escape for addressing the real issues, that approach will bring long-term damage to your relationship.

Buying a gift—The picture of a man bringing home a dozen roses to get himself out of the proverbial doghouse is familiar. It is true that sometimes a gift communicates love and, when given with sincere words, even apology for anger. But you cannot buy your way out of dealing with a conflict. Using a gift as a substitute for addressing the real problem or the issues between you cheapens your relationship over time.

Anger—The deception of anger is that sometimes an angry outburst will quiet the immediate conflict at hand. But this kind of "solving" conflict brings deeper harm to the relationship. James 1:20 tells us, "For the wrath of man worketh not the righteousness of God."

Another danger of anger is that it tends to escalate. One spouse lets out an angry outburst, and the other responds in kind. Proverbs 15:1 tells us how to break this vicious cycle: "A soft answer turneth away wrath: but grievous words stir up anger." If you continue to respond in anger, you continue to stir the anger in your spouse. But if you choose to humble yourself and respond with a soft answer, your words will begin to soften your spouse.

Our tendency to respond to conflict ineffectively—in any of the ten ways listed above—reminds me of the time I came home to find our youngest son Matthew playing with blocks on the floor. "Hey, Matt," I greeted him. "Are you building a house?"

His answer surprised me, and it immediately reminded me of many homes: "No, Dad, I don't know how to build a house. I can only build walls."

Without the help of the Holy Spirit, even well-meaning Christians are like Matt. We don't naturally know how to build a home; we build walls. But God's desire for your marriage is that you would take the blocks He has given to you—your words, actions, attitudes—and use them to build not walls, but a *home*.

RESPONDING WITH GRACE

Perhaps no area of our lives reveals our walk with the Lord like relational conflict, because these are the moments that our raw responses reveal the true depth of our development in Christlikeness. A spiritual Christian will take what seems like a large matter and make it smaller by responding properly. A carnal Christian, on the other hand, takes what could remain a small matter and makes it larger.

Another way to think of this is to pretend that everywhere you go you carry with you two buckets—one filled with gasoline and the other filled with water. The instances of conflict in your relationship are fires. Some are small fires, just a little spark. Some are large fires, threatening to destroy the relationship.

Your choice at each fire is from which bucket you will pour. Even a small fire will become large when gasoline is poured on it. And even a large fire can be put out when water is poured on it. The ineffective responses we have already mentioned are like gasoline, while spiritual, grace-filled responses are like water.

The good news is that God freely gives us His grace. Grace is the God-given desire and ability to please God. Philippians 2:13 says, "For it is God which worketh in you both to will and to do of his good pleasure." What does this grace look like during times of conflict?

Grace is listening to your spouse, rather than withdrawing or shooting back with cutting words.

> *Wherefore, my beloved brethren, let every man be swift to hear, slow to speak, slow to wrath:*—JAMES 1:19

Grace is bearing with your spouse's weaknesses rather than exploiting them and finding ways to "push his/her buttons."

> *We then that are strong ought to bear the infirmities of the weak, and not to please ourselves.*—ROMANS 15:1

Grace is being sensitive to the leading of the Holy Spirit when He prompts you to apologize for hurtful words or actions.

> *Let us therefore follow after the things which*
> *make for peace, and things wherewith one*
> *may edify another.*—ROMANS 14:19

Grace is taking time to seek God's wisdom together rather than relying on your own understanding when you have a difference of opinion.

> *Through wisdom is an house builded;*
> *and by understanding it is established.*
> —PROVERBS 24:3

Grace is being the one to suggest that you kneel together in prayer, asking God to help you work through your disagreement. (Don't forget that the oft-claimed verse below was given in the context of resolving disagreements.)

> *Again I say unto you, That if two of you*
> *shall agree on earth as touching any thing*
> *that they shall ask, it shall be done for*
> *them of my Father which is in heaven.*
> —MATTHEW 18:19

Grace is being courteous to your spouse when you feel insulted or hurt.

> *Finally, be ye all of one mind, having*
> *compassion one of another, love as brethren,*
> *be pitiful, be courteous:*—1 PETER 3:8

Grace is being willing to humble yourself to seek godly counsel when needed.

> *Likewise, ye younger, submit yourselves unto the elder. Yea, all of you be subject one to another, and be clothed with humility: for God resisteth the proud, and giveth grace to the humble.*—1 PETER 5:5

Grace is freely asking for and giving forgiveness, keeping a clean slate between you both.

> *And if he trespass against thee seven times in a day, and seven times in a day turn again to thee, saying, I repent; thou shalt forgive him.*—LUKE 17:4

Responding with grace is the result of humbling yourself before the Lord. It is the opposite of our natural response to conflict, which is to allow pride to rise up in our spirit in some form of self-protection or vindication. Pride is gasoline; humility is water.

Romans 12:18 instructs us to pour water: "If it be possible, as much as lieth in you, live peaceably with all men." You can't control your spouse, and you often can't control sources of conflict. But you can control your responses. Pour water.

CiTY OF PEACE

The last time Terrie and I were in Israel, we were leading a tour with a group from our church as well as friends of our ministry. As we arrived in Jerusalem, I noticed a strong police presence. The next day, as we toured the Old City of Jerusalem, I began to feel uneasy and told Terrie we may need to cut our time there short. Just an hour after we left, a bomb detonated near the area where we had been.

Although its very name means "City of Peace," Jerusalem has been a hotbed of violence and war over the centuries. Why is this? Primarily, it is on account of the Temple Mount—the most sacred piece of real estate on earth. Because Jews, Muslims, and Christians hold the Temple Mount as sacred, the entire city has become an ongoing location of conflict.

Think about this: the conflict that arises in Jerusalem isn't because the city is worthless, but because it is valuable. And so it is with your marriage. It is because of the value and significance of your relationship that Satan seeks to arouse conflict and desires to see you inflict wounds on one another.

What would happen if you each covenanted with the Lord and with each other that rather than fighting *against* each other, you would fight *with* the other to protect your marriage? What could happen if you determined that no conflict would be allowed to tear you apart from one another, but that you would instead use conflict as a reminder of the value of your marriage?

Conflict in marriage is inevitable. But it doesn't have to be a lifelong war. It can simply be a roadblock where two people, both filled with grace, work to navigate around it together.

(top) In front of
the Supreme Court,
Washington D.C.

(middle) The sign before
the roadblock in Hebron

(bottom) Abraham's
tomb in the background

(top) With our baskets of almond roses. You can see the joy in my eyes.

(middle) Terrie got a few roses handed out by herself before my announcement.

(bottom) Shopping together in Jerusalem just a few hours before the bomb detonated

SiX

TRAVELiNG LiGHT

Forgiveness

Airlines created their luggage restrictions for people like us. And if I use the word *us* generously (Terrie would tell you she does most of the overpacking), I also use it gratefully (Terrie also takes care of most of the packing).

In whichever mode of transportation we travel, we tend to pack to the maximum amount allowed. Or more.

A few years ago when we were in Italy with Larry, Ashley, and Ashley's parents, we traveled several hours by train between cities. Between the six of us on the trip, we had fifteen bags, plus Larry's favorite tripod. (Larry enjoys photography and videography, and his skill is the reason we have great pictures and video from family travel.)

European trains are not designed for American tourists who overpack. You only have a brief window of time to get on and off the train, so relaying multiple loads of luggage as we would have to do isn't especially feasible.

As soon as the train pulled into the station, we grabbed our bags, jumped on, and quickly filled every last nook and cranny. A few bags fit in the overhead compartments, some were stuffed behind our seats, and some had to be carried on our laps.

Getting the luggage positioned was the easy part. Getting it off in a similarly short amount of time proved to be more difficult. And in the end, we didn't do a good enough job. Although our suitcases with peanut butter and cheap souvenirs made it off the train, Larry's tripod got left behind—a casualty of overpacking.

THE HEAVIEST LUGGAGE

Overpacking is like that. It burdens those around you who find themselves pushing or carrying it, and you end up losing what is truly valuable.

Yet, Christian couples "overpack" all the time in their marriages. One spouse does something hurtful to the other, and the hurt spouse, rather than investing the energy and love to defuse the situation or heal the offense (as we discussed in the previous chapter), takes on the burden of anger and unforgiveness.

A wounded spirit, however, is always too heavy a burden to carry. Whether this load is composed of many small grudges that have built up over time or one monumental offense, it makes your relationship heavy and exhausting. Furthermore, a wounded spirit will burden those around you (especially those closest to you, such as your children) and cause you to lose that which is truly valuable—maybe even your marriage itself, maybe your walk with the Lord. Proverbs 18:14 warns, "The spirit of a man will sustain his infirmity; but a wounded spirit who can bear?" A wounded spirit is too heavy for you, and it is too heavy for your marriage.

Our thinking is tricky here, because we tend to believe that the reason we have the weights of bitterness or unforgiveness is because of what others have done to us. It is *their* fault—or *his* or *her* fault—that we struggle, right?

Jesus told His disciples, "It is impossible but that offences will come" (Luke 17:1). It is not a question of *if* your spouse will offend you, but *when*. No Christian is perfect, so no one is married to a perfect spouse. And imperfect spouses offend. *Every* marriage will have opportunity for bitterness. It is not so much the offense that is committed as it is our response as the offended that determines the emotional burden we carry.

Terrie and I both have our share of faults. In fact, during a recent getaway that Terrie and I took to celebrate our anniversary and evaluate our needs as a couple, I was convicted *(again)* of ways that I unintentionally hurt Terrie on a reoccurring basis—bringing stress home and having a demanding spirit. I have worked on these faults through the years, and have seen the Lord help me change, but they are an ongoing struggle.

Neither of us is perfect, but we have both been good forgivers. And that has made all the difference.

Do you want to travel lighter in your marriage? Learn to give grace for injury and kindness for anger. Become a good forgiver.

PROHIBITED ITEMS

If you travel by air, you'll see a list of prohibited items near security checkpoints in the airport. Some items—weapons, sharp objects, oversized equipment—are permitted for checked luggage but prohibited from carry-ons, while other items—blasting caps, dynamite, spillable batteries— are deemed hazardous and never allowed.

The Transportation Security Administration (TSA) doesn't always catch these prohibited items. Once when

Terrie and I were returning from a hunting trip in Montana, I had three bullets in my carry-on—a fact that I did not remember until we were in the middle of going through security. I held my breath as my bag went through the scanner and made a mental note to be more careful when it came out on the other side with the bullets undetected.

Although TSA cannot catch everything, God does see every aspect of our hearts. In Ephesians 4:31, He gives us a list of completely prohibited items for our relationships: "Let all bitterness, and wrath, and anger, and clamour, and evil speaking, be put away from you, with all malice." All six of the emotional responses on this list are hazardous to your heart and your marriage.

Let's look at each of these words and notice how any of them might appear in your relational luggage.

- **Bitterness** is from the Greek word *pikria,* and it means "acridity (especially poison), literally or figuratively." Think of an acid eating away at a solid, and you have a good picture of what bitterness does in a heart. Too many times I have seen a bitter spirit change the entire direction of a person's life and deeply affect those around them. We think that refusing to forgive proves we are the strong one in the relationship. But in reality, refusing to forgive makes us weak. An unknown author once wrote, "Unforgiveness is the poison we drink, hoping others will die." If you want to kill your marriage, bitterness is one of the surest ways to do it.

- **Wrath** is from the word *thumos,* and it means "passion (as if breathing hard)—fierceness, indignation, wrath." It speaks of the white-heat of a seething anger. If you go to bed angry, you will allow that anger to simmer in your heart, until it eventually boils over in other ways. You may not even frequently express it, but it is boiling under the surface of your relationship.

- **Anger** is from the word *orge* and means "violent passion—ire, or abhorrence; by implication punishment." This is the anger that blows up. Anger in general causes us to react to problems in the flesh rather than to respond in the Spirit. This is because our anger is usually self-centered—*our* feelings were hurt, *our* rights were violated, *our* efforts were unrecognized.

- **Clamor** is not a word we use often, but it is translated from the Greek word *krauge,* and it means, "an outcry." Perhaps the easiest present-day example of *clamor* is 90 percent of the "angry" posts on social media. They are usually more sound than substance and are much like a marital fight in which one or both spouses loosely toss threats or make dramatic claims to get the other's attention. One problem with clamor is that it never works. It usually just provokes the same or another type of anger from the other spouse.

- *Evil speaking* is from *blasphemia*, the same word often translated *blaspheme*. It means, "vilification (especially against God), evil speaking, railing." This sometimes takes place in person, but it is often slandering someone's name to others. It is the kind of talk that happens around the water cooler referring to "the old lady" or in the carpool complaining about how, "my husband just can't seem to...."

- *Malice* is from the word *kakia* and means "depravity... evil, wickedness." This is when your anger becomes meanness. It can happen when you actively plot revenge (refusing to speak, freezing a checking account, preparing food you know your spouse hates). But it can also happen when you passively accept sinfulness in your life, excusing it on your spouse's failure. I have too often heard spouses excuse an affair or an addiction to pornography in retaliation for "he/she doesn't meet my needs."

Unresolved anger in any of these forms will often fuel other sins. When a man harbors anger toward his wife, he may begin to justify immoral thoughts. When a woman harbors bitterness toward her husband, she may begin to look outside the marriage to get her emotional needs met.

Additionally, Ephesians 4:27 warns that anger literally helps Satan. In cautioning against allowing anger to linger in our relationships, Paul tells us, "Neither give place to the devil." No Christian wants to give Satan "place"—or a foothold—in their relationships. Yet when we allow anger to dwell in our hearts, we are giving Satan room to work.

Finally, anger almost always turns into a deep root of bitterness that adversely affects us as well as every relationship in our life. Hebrews 12:15 warns, "Looking diligently lest any man fail of the grace of God; lest any root of bitterness springing up trouble you, and thereby many be defiled." And 2 Corinthians 2:10–11 tells us that unforgiveness is one of the tactics of Satan to destroy our lives: "To whom ye forgive any thing, I forgive also: for if I forgave any thing, to whom I forgave it, for your sakes forgave I it in the person of Christ; *Lest Satan should get an advantage of us: for we are not ignorant of his devices.*"

This is why we must guard against anger and bitterness vigilantly. When we make small exceptions, we may find they burrow deep into our relationships and work destruction in ways we don't even realize.

Our family saw an illustration of this many years ago. We were in the middle of our first large building project for

Lancaster Baptist Church. Everything that could go wrong did, and even things that seemingly couldn't go wrong did. The stress was becoming overwhelming. My hair was falling out, my eyes were twitching, and, although I didn't want to admit it, I really needed to get away for a few days to rest.

Leo Walther, a man in his late 50s who had recently been saved, noticed. Leo had first come to our church, really in answer to his wife's many prayers over the years, but specifically to see his married son who we had been privileged to lead to Christ, get baptized. The Lord worked in Leo's heart, and within a couple more weeks, he also trusted Christ. God did a great work of grace in Leo's life. Shortly after being saved, he became convicted about the liquor store he owned, retired out of the business, and began volunteering full work weeks around the church.[1]

Leo approached me one day and said that he and Evelyn wanted to send our family to Wyoming where they often vacationed. Terrie and I have always been reluctant to accept a large gift from a church member. But after some insistence, we eventually accepted, and it turned out to be just what we needed.

We drove through Yellowstone National Park (the first time any of us had seen it), enjoyed blackberry milkshakes on the border of Utah and Wyoming, and finally arrived at the dude ranch where we would be staying near the Cheyenne River.

That week remains among our family's favorite memories. We went river rafting down the Cheyenne River (and almost lost five-year-old Matthew over the side of the raft), went horseback riding every day, and even got to visit the rodeo in Cody, Wyoming.

It was early June—just early enough in the year that there was still some snow on the mountains and just late enough in the year that the ticks were out. We didn't realize that until Larry and Matthew took their BB guns out to conquer the forest. When they returned, they were covered in ticks.

In case you're not familiar with ticks, allow me to share a few facts: They are external parasites that attach firmly to your skin and begin gorging on your blood. They are dangerous because they often carry diseases, and so they must be carefully pulled off one at a time, being sure that their head is not left in your body.

Terrie and I began pulling the ticks off Larry and Matt, and we realized that we would have to do daily tick checks.

Each night before bed, we checked the boys for ticks. Some ticks were just crawling, and we could flick them off. Others had to be pulled off. In either case, we couldn't let the ticks linger.

Every marriage also needs "tick checks." Think of anger and bitterness like parasites that will burrow into your relationship and cause great destruction. When you see the first signs of anger, don't let it stay on you. Whether you can simply flick it away or need to deal with it more thoroughly, take whatever steps necessary to do so.

God is specific in His instructions about what to do with anger: "Let all [forms of anger] be *put away* from you." Interestingly, the phrase *put away* is translated from one Greek word, *airo,* which means "to take up or away…lift up, loose." It gives the idea of *lightening your load.*

The way to travel heavy is to let an offense provoke anger in your heart and escalate into bitterness. The way to travel light is to learn to forgive.

HOW TO FORGIVE

Some people think of forgiveness as stuffing an offense out of sight, pretending it never happened. For instance, an unrepentant spouse may demand a "forgiveness" that never deals with the sin he or she committed against the other.

Biblical forgiveness, however, isn't stuffing an offense deep into your luggage. It is handing the offense over to God. It is trusting God to be the Judge and releasing your right to pass judgment.

This is why when Joseph's brothers, who had sinned deeply against him, were fearful that he would retaliate, Joseph replied, "Fear not: for am I in the place of God?" (Genesis 50:19). He wasn't saying that what they did when they sold him into slavery wasn't wrong; he was saying that it wasn't his place to make it right. This truth is echoed in Romans 12:19 when Paul writes to persecuted Christians, "Dearly beloved, avenge not yourselves, but rather give place unto wrath: for it is written, Vengeance is mine; I will repay, saith the Lord."

A forgiving Christian remembers that he, too, has been forgiven. In fact, Ephesians 4:32 reminds us of this as it instructs us: "...forgiving one another, *even as God for Christ's sake hath forgiven you.*" God did not forgive us because we were good people who had no sin. He forgave us "for Christ's sake"—because Jesus paid for our sins. Christians are not *good* people; we are *forgiven* people. It is because of the forgiveness we have been given that God *commands* us to forgive others in the same way He has forgiven us.

We think that our unwillingness to forgive is related to the size of the offense committed against us: If someone hurts me greatly, it is harder for me to forgive. But in reality, it is usually related to our *forgetfulness* of the forgiveness we have received. Pastor Martyn Lloyd-Jones wrote, "Whenever I see myself before God and realize something of what my blessed Lord has done for me at Calvary, I am ready to forgive anybody anything. I cannot withhold it. I do not even want to withhold it."

Jesus boiled forgiveness down to three basic steps: "If thy brother trespass against thee, rebuke him; and if he repent, forgive him. And if he trespass against thee seven times in a day, and seven times in a day turn again to thee, saying, I repent; thou shalt forgive him" (Luke 17:3–4). Rebuke, repent, forgive—let's look at all three.

Rebuke

"...rebuke him..."

The first response to an offense is to go directly to the person responsible and show him how he sinned against you. This may seem self-evident, but many couples don't do this. Depending on a person's personality, past, and the health of their current relationship, he may either hold the offense in or talk to someone else about it. *Both* of those responses are harmful to a relationship and become barriers to forgiveness. The simple rule from this verse is, don't talk *about* the person who hurt you, but do talk *to* him.

The question arises, who goes to the other first? When there has been an offense that turns into a standoff, should the one who was offended or the one who committed the offense go first? The answer is, *yes.*

In Matthew 5, Jesus instructs that if someone considers that you have wronged him ("that thy brother hath ought against thee"), you must go to him for reconciliation. In Matthew 18, Jesus says if someone does something against you ("if thy brother shall trespass against thee"), you are to go to him. Counselor Jay Adams explains, "There is never a time when you can sit and wait for your brother to come to you. Jesus doesn't allow for that. He gives no opportunity for that. It is always your obligation to go."[2]

God is not as interested in assigning blame as He is in solving the problem. The issue is not so much one of determining roles—who was hurt and who was the hurter—as it is facilitating reconciliation of the relationship. And this requires humility on the part of both parties. One person has to be humble enough to initiate.

Repentance
"...and if he repent..."

You've heard the statement, "When you forgive, you set two people free, and realize that one of them was yourself." The second part of this statement is definitely true. When you forgive someone, you release yourself from the acid of bitterness—even if that person never repents or receives your forgiveness. As we saw earlier, forgiveness isn't an option for a child of God. We are commanded to forgive as we have been forgiven.

But for true relational restoration to take place, the offender does need to repent. We see this in our relationship with God. Scripture tells us that God's posture toward us when we sin is that He is "ready to forgive" (Psalm 86:5). But it is not until we confess our sin—agree with God that what we have done is, in fact, sin—that we can receive God's forgiveness and have a fully restored relationship (1 John 1:9).

I have seen people who betrayed their spouse through an affair take an attitude of, "Look, I'm back. And you'd better forgive me, or it's your fault if our marriage doesn't heal." Even if the other spouse does forgive, a proud, non-repentant attitude cannot receive the forgiveness necessary for true relational restoration. There has to be a humble remorse over having committed sin against the other and a changing of the mind regarding that sin.

This isn't only true in what we consider "large" offenses in marriage. If I am harsh or belittling toward Terrie in little ways, but I never repent for it—I never genuinely apologize with remorse over how I hurt her—and simply expect her to go on forgiving, our relationship will be clouded by my sin toward her. Even if she keeps receiving God's grace to forgive me, my hardness of heart toward her will be a barrier in our marriage.

Most of us don't know how to ask for forgiveness. We hope to toss out a quick "I'm sorry if I was wrong" or go a little out of our way to atone by doing something extra. But to receive forgiveness, we have to humble ourselves to actually ask for it.

Years ago, I came across these "7 A's of Confession."[3] I have used these in counseling and at times to check my own sincerity in conveying repentance:

1. *Address everyone involved.* Only talk to people who are part of the problem or part of the solution.

2. *Avoid "if," "but," or "maybe."* Saying, "I know I shouldn't have yelled at you, but you were being really annoying" is just blaming the other person and finding fault with them for your failure. "I'm sorry if I offended you" is never a real apology.

3. *Admit specifically what you did.* If you know you have hurt your spouse but can't understand what you did, ask the Lord for wisdom and try to look at it through your spouse's eyes. If you still don't see it, ask your spouse (or a godly counselor) for help.

4. *Acknowledge the hurt.* Express sorrow for your sin. If it doesn't make you sad that you have hurt your spouse, it is going to be difficult for him or her to believe you want forgiveness, rather than a pass.

5. *Ask for forgiveness.* Some of the hardest words are "I'm sorry; I was wrong." But don't stop there. You must ask,

SIX—TRAVELING LIGHT / 135

"Will you forgive me?" These words, spoken in sincere humility, are powerful for restoring a relationship.

6. *Accept the consequences.* If there is any way you can make restitution, do. Don't demand your spouse pretend as if nothing has happened. Where trust has been broken—be it in a small or big way—your spouse may forgive you but needs evidence that he or she can trust you again.

7. *Alter your behavior.* You won't be perfect, but if you are genuinely sorry, you will give effort toward changing your behavior. Without real change, there is reason to question your repentance.

Once an offense has been confronted and apologized for, the next step is to freely give forgiveness.

Forgiveness
"...forgive him..."

Several years ago, Terrie and I had the privilege of preaching and teaching at a missionary retreat in Germany for missionaries from all over Europe. We thoroughly enjoyed our time with these men and women who sacrifice so greatly to spread the gospel in that region of the world. It was our privilege to teach on marriage, family life, and ministry during our time with them.

At the end of the conference, we took a day to see some of the sights of the area. Our first stop was the Neuschwanstein Castle, sometimes referred to as the "Disneyland Castle," because its fairy tale architecture inspired Walt Disney to create the Cinderella castle at the Magic Kingdom. The snow-capped mountains with the sun shining through surrounding the castle made it more than postcard beautiful.

About an hour's drive from the castle, we then arrived at the Dachau concentration camp. Our mood quickly changed from fairy tale happiness to grief and shock as we came face to face with the horrific realities of World War II and Adolf Hitler's hatred of the Jews.

We walked through the iron gate of the prisoners entrance which had words in it, reading, *"Arbeit macht frei"* or "Work will make you free." In reality, the people brought to Dachau, usually on severely overcrowded freight trains, were worked to death, starved, beaten, and treated in the most inhumane ways demented guards could think of.

We saw the bunks where prisoners slept in one of the thirty-two barracks, including a barrack reserved for medical experiments on humans. We saw the iron rods that had been used to beat prisoners. Near the back of the property we saw a large building, and our guide told us that as people went into that building, they were told they were getting a shower. Once inside, however, they quickly discovered they were in a gas chamber. We saw the crematoriums where the Nazis burned the bodies of those who died in the gas chambers or due to the extreme conditions of the camp. Those crematoriums, in fact, make the true number of how many were killed at Dachau unknown. We know of 32,000 people who lost their lives here, but we know there were thousands more.

While the gloom, despair, and even bitterness of those days still remain throughout the compound of Dachau and even in many lives, God's grace has abounded in many lives as well. Even people whose lives were shattered and hearts crushed through the monstrosities of the concentration camps have discovered that God's grace is greater than man's wickedness and that His grace gives them the ability to forgive.

One of the best known of these people is Corrie ten Boom, a Dutch Christian who helped her family hide Jews during the war. For this, she, her father, and her sister were imprisoned in Nazi concentration camps. Both her father and her sister died through the brutal treatment in the camps.

Years after the war, Corrie was speaking in a church about the love and forgiveness of God. After the service, a man came to thank her for her testimony. As he approached her, Corrie recognized him and recoiled. He had been one of the guards at Ravensbrück Camp.

He reached out his hand to shake hers, "A fine message! How good it is to know that our sins are at the bottom of the sea!"

She stood frozen.

"You mentioned Ravensbrück," he continued. "I was a guard there. But since that time, I have become a Christian. I know that God has forgiven me for the cruel things I did there, but I would like to hear it from your lips as well. Fräulein, will you forgive me?"

Corrie later described that moment: "I stood there with the coldness clutching my heart. But forgiveness is not an emotion—I knew that…. Forgiveness is an act of the will, and the will can function regardless of the temperature of the heart."[4]

She told how she reached out her hand to shake his, and *then* the love of God filled her heart.

You may think that you *can't* forgive your spouse because you have no feelings of forgiveness. God never instructs us to *feel* forgiveness; He instructs us to *give* forgiveness. As Corrie said, it is an act of the will.

Where there has been abuse or an affair or deeply entrenched patterns of purposeful hurt toward one another, you may need the help of a godly Christian leader or counselor, and never hesitate to get it. But even the goal of counseling should be for forgiveness and reconciliation.

Remember that God designed marriage as a picture of the gospel (Ephesians 5:31). That picture is not complete without forgiveness.

KEEP FORGIVING

When it comes to offenses and forgiveness, there are two kinds of people—scorekeepers and grace-givers.

The disciple Peter started out as a scorekeeper. Right after Jesus taught His disciples about forgiveness, Peter asked the question we all remember: "Lord, how oft shall my brother sin against me, and I forgive him? till seven times?" (Matthew 18:21).

You can almost hear the incredulous tone in Peter's voice. "Until *seven times?*" It's as if he thought he was suggesting the extreme limit of forgiveness. Peter wanted to keep track like a scorekeeper at a basketball game. He wanted to say, "I will forgive up until a certain point. But once you cross the line, I'm released of my obligation to forgive."

Jesus' answer changed the game: "I say not unto thee, Until seven times: but, Until seventy times seven" (Matthew 18:22).

If I could paraphrase, Jesus said, "Peter, forget the scoreboard. Forgive."

Peter, don't be a scorekeeper; be a grace-giver.

If you've read the epistles of 1 and 2 Peter, you know that Peter did become a grace-giver. And he learned it from Jesus Himself.

> For even hereunto were ye called: because Christ also suffered for us, leaving us an example, that ye should follow his steps: Who did no sin, neither was guile found in his mouth: Who, when he was reviled, reviled not again; when he suffered, he threatened not; but committed himself to him that judgeth righteously: Who his own self bare our sins in his own body on the tree, that we, being dead to sins, should live unto righteousness: by whose stripes ye were healed.—1 PETER 2:21–24

No one wins when you keep score against your spouse. Not you, not your spouse.

If you want to be a good forgiver, you must learn to be a grace-giver. Give grace—and give it persistently.

PACKING SKILLS

If anger and bitterness are too heavy to carry, with what are we to replace them? Directly following the verse telling us to put off anger in all its forms, Ephesians 4:32 provides a short list: "And be ye kind one to another, tenderhearted, forgiving one another, even as God for Christ's sake hath forgiven you."

Kindness, tenderheartedness, forgiveness—these are the skills of great forgivers.

- **Kind** is from the Greek word *chrestos*, and it means "employed, useful…good(-ness), gracious." It gives the idea of busying yourself to help others. New Testament kindness isn't simply the absence of meanness; it is the presence of useful goodness.

- **Tenderhearted** is from the word *eusplagchnos*. It means "well compassioned, i.e., sympathetic —pitiful." It means that you keep a soft heart toward others, even those who have hurt you.

- **Forgiving** is from the word *charizomai*, and it means, "to grant as a favor…pardon or rescue." Its very definition underscores that forgiveness is a voluntary act of the will rather than a reflex of the emotions.

These are not single actions—they are skills. These are actions we must repeat over and over and over and yet again if we want a relationship free of the baggage of anger and bitterness.

I mentioned at the beginning of this chapter that Terrie and I are not perfect. We both have our faults. And sometimes when we step back to look at the things that we tend to struggle with in our marriage, it's disheartening to see how we need to forgive each other for the same things again and again.

And yet, at the same time, it's heartening to realize that God has given us grace to do this for thirty-six years. No, we're not perfect, but we have become very good forgivers.

THE FREEDOM OF FORGIVENESS

This past summer, Terrie and I met Rouguo, a schoolteacher in Germany who lived in East Berlin after World War II. We met Rouguo because, although she is a teacher, she works as a tourist guide on the weekend, simply because she doesn't want the history of what her country endured to be forgotten.

Rouguo told us what it was like to be a child under Soviet rule in East Germany. She told us about the hunger and poverty she lived in. She described the government's absolute control over citizens' private lives and the fear people lived under. She told us how she had wanted to study languages, but when it came time for university, she wasn't allowed to choose—the Soviets told her what she would study.

But, as we stood in front of the Brandenburg Gate, Rouguo told us about the day that very gate opened. When she, as a young college-age adult, walked through that gate into West Germany for the first time, she was in shock. All the color! The food, the choices, the freedom! She just couldn't take it all in.

We asked Rouguo, "How did realizing all you had missed make you feel? Are you angry? Bitter?"

Her answer was immediate and definite. "No, I'm just grateful that now I have the opportunity to be free and to share with others what freedom means."

Rouguo could have let the past hardships she had experienced ruin the rest of her life. She could have remained imprisoned to the past through bitterness. But she chose to forgive. And because of that choice, she is passing on a piece of history like no one else I have ever met.

As Christians, we know that our ultimate freedom is found in Christ and the forgiveness He offers us (a message we were able to share with Rouguo as well). But we can't fully enjoy that freedom as long as we are bound by unforgiveness toward another person.

Could I encourage you that whatever the past has been in your relationship that you would release it through forgiveness? When you become a good forgiver, the journey is lighter.

(top) Copenhagen, Denmark

(middle) Wyoming vacation, 1993

(top left) Neuschwanstein Castle, Germany ("Disneyland Castle")

(top right) Dachau—It was hard to believe these two locations were just an hour apart.

(above) This charming Christmas shop was just blocks away from Dachau. It is incredible to reflect on the civilians who lived in this area during the war and carried out their lives as if the brutality that was taking place behind Dachau's gates wasn't happening.

(right) Brandenburg Gate, through which Rouguo and others eventually walked to freedom.

SEVEN
BOOKiNG A ROOM
Intimacy

We're not really camping people. So when we were told we needed to bring sleeping bags to a missionary conference we had been asked to speak at in Central America, we had to make a run to Big 5 to buy two. Also, because we are not camping people, we didn't know that sleeping bags are rated for outside temperature. So when we left the store with two Alaskan sleeping bags, we had no idea what we had just done to ourselves.

A few days later, we arrived in Costa Rica at the camp where the conference was to be held and where we would be staying. Nestled in that gorgeous scenery such as is found throughout Central and South America, the camp itself was more rustic than we had anticipated. Across the street was a large chicken farm, which provided a permeating perfume as well as early morning wake-up calls. The doorways and window frames to each cabin were open—as in, there were no doors or windows, and the iguanas seemed to appreciate the easy access into the rooms and chapel. Our hosts handed us bottles of water with stern instructions not to touch the water in the sinks.

The conference itself was refreshing. It was a joy to hear what God was doing through mission works across Central America, and it was our privilege to be able to serve the missionaries gathered for the conference.

Each night, however, was excruciating. Even after the sun went down, the heat and humidity were overwhelming. And that, without being in a subzero sleeping bag, as we decided to sleep on top of our sleeping bags instead of inside them. That idea, however, lost its sparkle when we turned the lights out, and the flying cockroaches came to life. With no covering, we were easy, frequent targets. Our next solution was to unfasten the curtains from the empty window frames and use them as sheets. That helped, but it's hard to relax with cockroaches falling on you, even if you do have a curtain between you and the unrelenting pests. We woke up each morning tense and unrested.

We did, however, enjoy a short moment of revenge on the cockroaches the first morning at breakfast, as we watched a hefty roach fall into a large pot on the stove. But when a distracted cook stirred him in, our appetite died along with the roach. So in the end, the cockroaches still had the last laugh.

Besides sweet memories of the time spent with missionaries during the conference, an additional blessing of this trip was that we got to know missionary Ed Bordell, who has served in Costa Rica now for over twenty-five years. He noticed we were struggling, and each evening, after he drove into town, he would bring us Diet Coke and cookies from McDonald's. (When you're in a foreign country, McDonald's always seems like comfort food, even if it's not your restaurant of preference in the States.)

As the conference came to a close, I mentioned to Ed that we had an extra day before our flight would leave and asked if he knew of a nice hotel where we could go to get some rest before heading home. He told us the roads were so bad we would spend many hours just driving and suggested instead that we catch a flight. In fact, he knew someone who knew someone who could take us on a private plane that very afternoon. He made reservations for us at a hotel, and we went to bed that last night eagerly anticipating our trip the next day.

The plane was small—it was all cockpit, but the pilot got us both in. Terrie gets nervous flying anyway, and tiny planes do little to ease her nerves. This one had an added layer of worry in that all of the gauges across the flight deck were empty. Literally. There were empty round sockets with no dials. Our pilot spoke no English and we spoke no Spanish, so he was spared our questions. We held each other's hands and hoped we had done well to trust Ed.

Pretty soon we were flying above beautiful rain forest-covered mountains. The scenery was breathtaking...as was our landing. We watched the pilot begin his descent with nothing below us except jungle and beach. No airport, no runway, no sign of civilization whatsoever. Using the beach as a runway, the pilot swooped down, stopped the plane, and, leaving the engine still running, motioned for us to exit. And then he took off again, leaving us stranded with the ocean on one side, the jungle on the other, and a rusty sign that read "WATCH FOR LOW FLYING AIRCRAFT." We didn't know what to do, so we sat on our suitcases and sleeping bags by the jungle and waited.

About an hour later, we heard what sounded like a lawnmower. Soon, a four-wheeler appeared from the jungle, and the driver motioned for us to get on. He, too, spoke no English, but he made us understand that he would take us to the hotel.

Relief washed over us. We could hardly wait to get to an air-conditioned room and get out of our sweat-drenched clothes. When we reached the front desk to ask for our room, the clerk told us the hotel was full.

"No problem," I told them. "We have a reservation. Paul Chappell," I spoke slowly, the way you do when you're trying to speak through a language barrier.

The man flipped through his reservation book. "No, señor, I am very sorry. But we have no room for you."

We were beside ourselves. We had no way to communicate in anything other than slowed-down English. We had no transportation. We were hours away from anybody we knew. We were foreigners stranded in a foreign country. And we were drenched in sweat, to boot.

"Look again," I pleaded. "I know my friend told me he made a reservation for us. The name is Paul Chappell." This time I said it even more slowly, more deliberately, emphasizing each sound.

"We are very sorry, señor. But all of our rooms are full."

Fortunately, I had Ed Bordell's phone number with me. I gave it to the clerk to call and listened to a one-sided conversation in Spanish, straining to catch words I might understand. We watched as the clerk shook his head, listened, looked back at his notebook...and then a broad smile. He turned to me, "Oh, sí, Señor *Raul* Chappell. We have a room for you."

P or *R*—the difference of one letter almost kept us from a room.

That trip to Costa Rica may not have turned out anything like what we anticipated, but it was an adventure we will never forget. It taught us to expect the unexpected, enjoy the detours, and check the temperature rating of sleeping bags.

Far more significant in a marriage, however, than a single trip or a single hotel room is the ongoing physical intimacy between a husband and a wife. And like our stay in Costa Rica, this area of a couple's life is often full of expectations (sometimes unrealistic), surprises, and adventure.

Marital intimacy is a key component of the weaving together that we looked at in chapter 1 and is the primary implication of Adam and Eve becoming "one flesh." God designed this intimacy to be the celebration of oneness and unity and the ongoing consummation of love between a husband and a wife.

Like everything good and holy that God creates, Satan works to exploit it by creating counterfeits—corruptions of the real thing. This is why although sex is one of God's great gifts of marriage, it can also be an area of confusion, misunderstanding, sin, and pain.

In this chapter, we will look at this gift as God created it as well as noting some common misuses of it.

EXCLUSIVE RESORT

Within the context of marriage, God designed intimacy to be wonderful and satisfying: "Drink waters out of thine own cistern, and running waters out of thine own well....Let thy fountain be blessed: and rejoice with the wife of thy youth. Let her be as the loving hind and pleasant roe; let her breasts satisfy thee at all times; and be thou ravished always with her love" (Proverbs 5:15, 18–19).

But God also warns that if you step outside of marriage to indulge in sexual activity, the wounds will be real and lasting. Throughout the book of Proverbs, Solomon highlights the dangers of being seduced by the lie that sex outside of marriage will bring nothing more than immediate pleasure. The truth is, it will bring terrible and lasting pain: "For the lips of a strange woman drop as an honeycomb, and her mouth is smoother than oil: But her end is bitter as wormwood, sharp as a twoedged sword. Her feet go down to death, her steps take hold on hell" (Proverbs 5:3–5).

Why the deep regret, shame, and wounds from sexual sins? Sex is more than just a physical act; it entwines two souls as well. When this happens within marriage, it is a great gift of God. When it happens outside of marriage, it becomes a sin against your own body. The apostle Paul wrote about this as he instructed the church at Corinth, a city that openly celebrated sexual sin, to turn from these sins: "What? know ye not that he which is joined to an harlot is one body? for two, saith he, shall be one flesh.... Flee fornication. Every sin that a man doeth is without the body; but he that committeth fornication sinneth against his own body" (1 Corinthians 6:16, 18).

Sexual love is like fire in that when it is built and confined in one location, it brings warmth and heat. It is pleasurable and useful. But when it has no boundaries around it, it brings destruction and death. Without boundaries, it ravages lives and families.

To protect the sacredness of marital intimacy, God has directly forbidden sexual practices that undermine what He designed for intimacy to be. These prohibitions are not meant to *limit* our pleasure, but to *enhance* it. They are boundaries for the protection of sex as the good gift it is. Notice these six categories:[1]

- Sex outside of marriage: adultery, fornication (1 Corinthians 6:16–18, 7:1; Galatians 5:19; Hebrews 13:4)
- Sex relations with a member of the same sex: homosexuality (Leviticus 18:22; Romans 1:27–28)
- Sex relations with a member of your family: incest (Leviticus 18:6–18)
- Sex fantasies or desires for someone other than your spouse, which amounts to adultery in God's sight; pornography of any kind, as well as mentally playing out lustful fantasies for real or imaginary women or men (Matthew 5:27–28; Galatians 5:19; Colossians 3:5)

- Sex that finds pleasure in pain or violence: rape, sadomasochism, brutality (1 Corinthians 7:5; Colossians 3:5; 1 Thessalonians 4:3–6)
- Sex that involves body parts not designed by God for intercourse: sodomy (Romans 1:24, 6:12–13)

Physical intimacy outside of marriage, as well as any sexual practices that are unholy, are hurtful to you as well as to your spouse. You are joined together in a covenant of oneness, and you honor one another by treating intimacy as a pure, sacred act that can bring glory to God and deep, mutual enjoyment with one another.

FiVE-STAR HOTEL

For our church's annual marriage retreat we often choose a five-star hotel. We could get a less expensive rate at a two-star location, but we know that a higher rating means there will be higher values in room comfort and staff service. In fact, most five-star hotels or resorts have their core values for guest care and customer service posted in their lobby. The better articulated and followed these values are by the management and staff, the better your stay will be. (And the more likely you are to return.)

Marital intimacy also has core values that contribute to its quality. Without these biblical values, intimacy is reduced to an act of selfishness. With these qualities, it is a celebration of one another and marriage. These qualities are purity, passion, and love.

Purity

Our world has so perverted sex, not only through the porn industry, but by sexualizing *everything*—down to kids' clothes and making *sexy* an acceptable, common-use adjective. The net result of this sexualization is removing the sacredness of marital intimacy.

Remember, however, that marital sex as God designed it isn't just pleasurable; it is also sacred and honorable. Within marriage, it is *awesome;* outside of marriage, it is damaging. Hebrews 13:4 presents both sides to this: "Marriage is honourable in all, and the bed undefiled: but whoremongers and adulterers God will judge."

So, what does purity look like *within* marriage? Another way to ask this is, if you are already married, does that mean anything goes between you and your spouse? In the book *Marriage on the Rock,* author Jimmy Evans provides helpful questions to consider in relation to sexual acts between a husband and a wife:[2]

- Does this increase oneness and intimacy?
- Is it mutually pleasurable or at least mutually agreed upon? (Spouses should not be forced to do anything against their wills.)[3]

- Is it hygienically and physically safe?
- Can I do this with a clear conscience before God? (God is not a prude, and He is not embarrassed by sex. However, according to Scripture, if we cannot do something by faith, it is sin.)[4]
- Is this something I would want my children to practice in their marriages someday?

But there is more to purity than just what you do together as a couple. There is the guarding of your own mind and actions. Paul instructed Timothy, "Keep thyself pure" and "Flee also youthful lusts: but follow righteousness..." (1 Timothy 5:22, 2 Timothy 2:22).

In our marriage counseling experience, we have encountered two common enemies to purity. One tends more toward men and the other more toward women, but we have seen either spouse struggle with both. In this section, we'll address these issues from their most common perspective, but realize that either of you could struggle with either one of these.

For men, the issue is often lust that is stirred through pornography. We live in such a pornographic age in which porn is not only accessible, but, incredibly, it is rationalized. (*Everyone does it. I can't help it. This is just a normal guy thing.*)

Not only is porn ungodly because it tarnishes your mind and exploits other people in the making of it, but it is damaging to you and your spouse because it is unrealistic. When young men receive their information about sex through locker room talk and glossy images in a magazine or on a screen, they have a fake view of sexuality. They then expect their spouse to look or act in ways that are absolutely unrealistic. Pornography is a fantasy world that cheapens your spouse. It causes men to *use* their wives rather than to *love* them. It makes even the sex that does happen within marriage selfish rather than wholesome; it makes it about gratification rather than about intimacy, with intimacy a sort of unintentional byproduct.

I have counseled couples in which the husband not only indulged in pornography himself, but he would ask his wife to look at trash as well. If this is you, please understand that what you are doing is a sin against God and against your spouse. You are to nourish and cherish your wife—to protect her and to love her as you love your own body (Ephesians 5:28–29). To ask your wife to look with you at inappropriate images or to compare her to other women is terribly degrading and dishonoring.

Porn is designed to cloud purity. It ignites impure thoughts that lead you to fantasize outside the will of God and to respond sexually to someone besides your spouse. Listen to the words of Jesus about this: "But I say unto you, That whosoever looketh on a woman to lust after her hath committed adultery with her already in his heart" (Matthew 5:28).

Tragically, with the growth of the Internet, porn has become increasingly accessible, as it is just a few clicks away and offers a promise of secrecy. Online secrecy, however, is an illusion. Regardless of where immoral behavior takes place, it will become exposed and bring destruction to a man's life. Proverbs 9:16–18 warns of secret sexual sin: "Whoso is simple, let him turn in hither: and as for him that wanteth understanding, she saith to him, Stolen waters are sweet, and bread eaten in secret is pleasant. But he knoweth not that the dead are there; and that her guests are in the depths of hell."

If you engage in pornography at any level, you must get out. And, as with any sin that thrives in secrecy, you will need help. Talk to your pastor, to a godly man twenty or more years older than you, to someone who can help you break free.[5] And know that freedom is available. Titus 2:11–12 tells us that God's grace teaches us to deny ungodliness and worldly lusts, but to be able to live righteously and godly "in this present world." And in a world that is so full of temptation, that last phrase is encouraging.

If men struggle with lust, women struggle as the victims of it. The tragic statistics are that as high as 50 percent of women have endured some form of sexual abuse or assault, and often as a child.[6] The impact of sexual abuse is profound emotional pain, often including confusion as well as a sense of guilt and shame. Sometimes teenagers or young adults fight this pain by becoming promiscuous. Others struggle with fear and, even after marriage, with a paralyzing inability to respond sexually.

If you have suffered abuse, you will almost certainly need the help of a godly counselor who can guide you in seeing, from God's perspective, what was done to you and how to find healing through His grace. Until you recognize that what was done to you was first, a sin and second, not your fault, you will not be able to free yourself from it through forgiveness. (Also, although forgiveness will be necessary for your own healing, that forgiveness does not mean that you don't report to authorities someone who has committed a crime. This is important particularly to keep a perpetrator from having access to more victims.)

You will also need to be able to share with your husband what was done to you as you both work through its results together. If your spouse was sexually abused, I would encourage you to offer compassion and love and then to do your best to understand the effects of that abuse on your spouse.

These are heavy topics, and the space they deserve is greater than the pages we have been able to give them. If either of these topics touch on issues that you deal with, I would encourage you to purchase and read the applicable books I've footnoted as well as to prayerfully seek biblical help.

God does not take sexual perversions lightly, nor does He stand aloof from those who have suffered by them. The verses below can be helpful in both motivating you to walk in purity as well as in understanding God's heart for your healing if you stand on either side of these issues:

> *For this is the will of God, even your sanctification, that ye should abstain from fornication: That every one of you should know how to possess his vessel in sanctification and honour; Not in the lust of concupiscence, even as the Gentiles which know not God: That no man go beyond and defraud his brother in any matter: because that the Lord is the avenger of all such, as we also have forewarned you and testified. For God hath not called us unto uncleanness, but unto holiness.*—1 THESSALONIANS 4:3–7

Passion

If you ever wonder if God really designed for marriage to include sexual passion, go ahead and read Song of Solomon, especially chapter 4 describing the wedding night between Solomon and his bride:

Behold, thou art fair, my love; behold, thou art fair; thou hast doves' eyes within thy locks: thy hair is as a flock of goats, that appear from mount Gilead. Thy teeth are like a flock of sheep that are even shorn, which came up from the washing; whereof every one bear twins, and none is barren among them. Thy lips are like a thread of scarlet, and thy speech is comely: thy temples are like a piece of a pomegranate within thy locks. Thy neck is like the tower of David builded for an armoury, whereon there hang a thousand bucklers, all shields of mighty men. Thy two breasts are like two young roes that are twins, which feed among the lilies. Until the day break, and the shadows flee away, I will get me to the mountain of myrrh, and to the hill of frankincense. Thou art all fair, my love; there is no spot in thee. Come with me from Lebanon, my spouse, with me from Lebanon: look from the top of Amana, from the top of Shenir and Hermon, from the lions' dens, from the mountains of the leopards. Thou hast ravished my heart, my sister, my spouse; thou hast ravished my heart with one of thine eyes, with one chain of thy neck. How fair is thy love, my sister, my spouse! how much better is thy love than wine! and the smell of thine ointments than

*all spices! Thy lips, O my spouse, drop as
the honeycomb: honey and milk are under
thy tongue; and the smell of thy garments is
like the smell of Lebanon. A garden inclosed
is my sister, my spouse; a spring shut up, a
fountain sealed. Thy plants are an orchard
of pomegranates, with pleasant fruits;
camphire, with spikenard, Spikenard and
saffron; calamus and cinnamon, with all
trees of frankincense; myrrh and aloes, with
all the chief spices: A fountain of gardens,
a well of living waters, and streams from
Lebanon. Awake, O north wind; and come,
thou south; blow upon my garden, that the
spices thereof may flow out. Let my beloved
come into his garden, and eat his pleasant
fruits.*—SONG OF SOLOMON 4:1–16

Set into Eastern poetry, some of the wording may
be different than what you say in your bedroom, but the
passion isn't. God *created* our bodies to enjoy sexual arousal
as a married couple. Passion is not an unholy thing; it is a
sacred thing.

One of the most helpful aspects of intimacy for both
husbands and wives to understand is that arousal for each
comes in different ways. Men are more visually stimulated,
and women are more gently stimulated. You can even see
this throughout the book of Song of Solomon. During

their wedding night in chapter 4 as well as their continued times of making love, Solomon is gentle and tender leading up to and after sex. He begins slowly by describing (with increasing passion) to his bride how beautiful she is to him, gently touching her, and kissing. She responds to his tenderness, enjoying these moments as much as he does. Song of Solomon 4:16 are the only words in this chapter by Solomon's wife: *"Awake, O north wind; and come, thou south; blow upon my garden, that the spices thereof may flow out. Let my beloved come into his garden, and eat his pleasant fruits."*

Misunderstanding and dissatisfaction come when a husband or wife assumes that their spouse is aroused in the same way they are. A husband who doesn't understand his wife's need for gentleness will cause his wife to feel used and frustrated. Similarly, a wife who doesn't understand her husband's need for frequency and visual stimulation will cause her husband to feel degraded and unloved.

A difference between men and women in intimacy that took me (Terrie) some time to understand is the setting. Most women prefer a romantic setting and a perfect moment to unwind and celebrate their marriage. Most men, however, find sex to be a great way to unwind, even during stressful seasons of life. Understanding the difference has helped us be more understanding of one another's needs. From a personal perspective, this understanding has also helped me to anticipate my husband's needs and given me a greater desire to create romance to make these times enjoyable and satisfying for both of us.

Aside from special times of fasting or physical need, marital intimacy is to be regular between husband and wife. Intimacy is not only a sacred act of celebrating oneness; it is a sacred trust in which you are making your body available to your spouse.

> *Let the husband render unto the wife due benevolence: and likewise also the wife unto the husband. The wife hath not power of her own body, but the husband: and likewise also the husband hath not power of his own body, but the wife. Defraud ye not one the other, except it be with consent for a time, that ye may give yourselves to fasting and prayer; and come together again, that Satan tempt you not for your incontinency.*
> —1 CORINTHIANS 7:3–5

With these thoughts in mind, I'd like to provide several practical but general tips for Christian couples related to passion and lovemaking.[7]

1. The marriage bed is to be a place of honor between couples. We saw this already from Hebrews 13:4, but I want to emphasize here that a couple should pray for

God's strengthening in their marriage, including the intimacy He has given to them. Much of the following points is the practical outflow of this truth.

2. Couples should avoid a preconceived idea of "the ultimate experience." Young couples may need time to learn each other and how to please each other.

3. Intercourse is designed by God as an expression of love. If couples would treat each other all through marriage the way they do on their honeymoon, it would greatly enhance their lovemaking.

4. Regular date times and remembering special occasions will make deposits into your spouse's heart that are remembered during intimate moments, making sexual intimacy the celebration of a fuller love and drawing both spouses' hearts toward one another during it. You cannot be harsh toward or condemning of one another in the afternoon and expect unselfish lovemaking in the evening.

5. A husband and wife should work to maintain a positive attitude toward their intimate life. Lovemaking is not primarily about one's looks as much as one's attitude toward marriage and their spouse's needs.

6. A husband should love his wife for who she is as a person. Often we hear woman say, "He is only nice to me when he wants sex."

7.   A husband should not use crude phrases from society to express feelings to his wife in bed. This feels degrading to her, even though he may mean it to be a compliment.

8.   A husband should learn to be slow and gentle in his caresses. If two people love each other and control themselves patiently while giving satisfaction to their spouse, they will learn how to please one another and find mutual enjoyment during these times.

9.   Gentle touches communicate approval, acceptance, and love. Song of Solomon 2:6 and 8:3 speak of a wife's desire for her husband's embrace.

10. God instructs a husband to dwell with his wife "according to knowledge, giving honour unto the wife..." (1 Peter 3:7). Learn her needs, be aware of her health, and be willing to show honor to both.

11. Verbal kindness and compliments from a husband in both nonsexual and intimate moments are critical for a wife to feel responsive during intimate moments.

12. Absolute privacy is vital. This is true of physical privacy during lovemaking, and it is also true of subject privacy at all times. Neither a husband nor a wife should discuss intimacy of their marriage with anyone else. (The only exception may be with joint consent for counseling.)

13. Foreplay, or loveplay, is essential in unselfish lovemaking. Thirty minutes or so actually allows both partners the emotional and physical readiness for intimacy. This can include gently massaging and touching.

14. A wife should verbally coach her husband to her needs. As a husband touches his wife intimately, she can encourage him with acts of cooperation or posturing in ways that signal to him her approval.

15. Kindness should always prevail in lovemaking. Even in times of forceful physical motions, love is shown in kindness.

Love

The most well-known passage on love in Scripture is 1 Corinthians 13. We already looked at this passage in relation to the larger picture of committed love in marriage. But take a moment to read its core verses again, applying these to the love expressed during marital intimacy.

> *Charity suffereth long, and is kind; charity envieth not; charity vaunteth not itself, is not puffed up, Doth not behave itself unseemly, seeketh not her own, is not easily provoked, thinketh no evil; Rejoiceth not in iniquity, but rejoiceth in the truth; Beareth all things, believeth all things,*

hopeth all things, endureth all things.
—1 CORINTHIANS 13:4–7

Love in the bedroom is more than the act of sex itself. It is also kindness, purity, and sacrifice toward your spouse. It is being willing to give of your body in a way that turns on the passions and meets the needs of your spouse as well as honoring your spouse's preferences, conscience, and needs.

From a standpoint of time spent, marital intimacy is just a fraction of marital love. It is the consummation of love, not the totality of it. Because love is much larger than the bedroom, it is so important that you keep your love toward one another alive and active, not only in how you practice intimacy, but also in every other aspect of your relationship.

HERE BY THE FIRELIGHT

In our home, we have a fireplace in the living room. During the fall and winter months, the fireplace is a great place to enjoy one another's company.

We noted at the beginning of this chapter that sexual love is like fire in that it is pleasurable within marriage, but destructive outside of marriage. But if you continue reading Song of Solomon, you'll discover love and fire are alike in another way as well. Perhaps the most famous verse of this book is found in its last chapter: "Many waters cannot quench love, neither can the floods drown it" (8:7).

What is interesting about the passion that Solomon describes here is that many years have passed since the beginning of their relationship. They are now in the twilight years of life, and yet, their passion for one another is still strong.

Why are they still in love? How can that be possible?

Remember Solomon and his wife's wedding night in Song of Solomon 4 as they both invested passion into the consummation of their marriage? Throughout the remaining chapters of Song of Solomon, you'll find that this couple continued to stoke the fire. They had their moments of disagreement, but they made up...and they continued to enjoy physical expressions of love.

Marital intimacy needs the continuing investment of both spouses. It needs the husband to put logs on the fire by showing gentleness and kindness—continuing to give verbal compliments and frequent expressions of love, both inside and outside of the bedroom. And it needs the wife to also stoke the fire—to encourage and respond to her husband's passion, to give time and attention to all of his needs.

Some couples grow more distant the longer they are married. But this need not be if they will continue to keep the fire of their love burning for one another—and take time to rekindle it as needed.

When Terrie and I reach the twilight years of our lives, we want to still be here by the fireplace. For this to happen, we both continue to purposefully stoke the flames.

(top) A rainy day in Saint Andrews, Scotland

(bottom) At the missionary conference in Costa Rica. If you look closely, you can see the Diet Coke bottle in front of Terrie.

EiGHT
TOURiST TRAP
Contentment

For our twenty-fifth anniversary of serving at Lancaster Baptist Church, our church family gave us an incredibly generous gift—a family vacation to anywhere we would like to visit.

Our youngest son, Matt, had been married for less than a year, but it was long enough that his wife, Katie, had heard about the vacations we took when our children were all little—Cayucos, California. If you Google *Cayucos* now, you'll read that it is a "beach resort town." It's actually a town of 2,500 people, and it was even smaller twenty-five years ago. We went there because no one else was there and we could get an inexpensive motel room for a week. We would buy bread and deli meat at the grocery store and go on walks together for entertainment.

Truly, some of our most precious family memories are at Cayucos, and neither Terrie nor I regret a single vacation we took there. But you had to be there to appreciate it, and Katie wasn't there back then. So she lobbied for something more exotic—Spain.

We compared our calendars, searched for tickets, and planned an itinerary. I researched the historical significance of the places we would see and prepared three-ring binders—one for each family member—with my findings. (I always think if you're going to go somewhere where you have never been and may never see again, you should squeeze every bit of historical and geographical significance possible out of it. Terrie thinks you should enjoy rest in new surroundings. We still travel a little differently.) Even though we were traveling with our four married children and their spouses, Terrie, as usual, packed suitcases of peanut butter and snacks. And we were off.

A few days later, while at the Rock of Gibraltar, we realized that we were just a ferry ride away from Morocco. Most of our family had never been to Africa, so a day trip to Tangier, the nearest Moroccan city, sounded fun.

Unlike the rest of our trip, where we had researched ahead and planned for guides where needed, we were on our own once we got off the ferry. We don't know Arabic, and, other than just enjoying a day in Africa, we didn't have a clue what we wanted to do or see. In other words, we were prime targets for locals who make their living off tourists.

As we made our way to downtown Tangier, a local man offered to be our guide. He had a badge, and we needed a guide, so we paid him and followed where he led. His English was minimal, but he did a great job showing us around. He even brought us to the camel ride merchant, and we all had a turn.

In a seeming flash of inspiration, he asked if we would like to see a snake charmer. Our kids, in particular, were loving this spur-of-the-moment, freedom-from-research-binders day. Before any of us really had a chance to talk about if we should see a snake charmer, Katie spoke up for us all: "Yes!"

And just like that, our newfound guide turned off the main road and led us into a side street. From the side street, he took us down a narrow alley where unevenly-set brick apartment buildings lined both sides. Cats roamed the trash in the gutters, and you could touch the buildings on either side while standing in the center. It was the kind of place your mother would warn you not to go.

We followed our guide single file through a few turns until he stopped at one of the cloth-draped doorways and called out something in Arabic. A man appeared wearing an embroidered hat and holding a writhing pillowcase. He reached in and pulled out the largest cobra I had ever seen other than on a flat screen. And he was less than a yard away from us.

Terrie and I jumped back as our guide's snake-charmer friend tried to assure us in broken English that his snakes really were harmless and would be perfectly obedient to him. He set his cobra down, turned on his music, and the snake danced to it.

He must have been able to tell that we had had enough and were eying our escape options, because he reached into his pillowcase again and pulled out another snake. This one he began wrapping around Katie's neck.

We've encountered tourist traps before, but this tops them all as the most unusual. Here we were, trapped in the back alley corner of a city we didn't know, where people spoke a language we couldn't understand, and surrounded by strangers and snakes—and it was all due to wanting to see and experience more…more than we responsibly could.

Discontentment is something like a tourist trap. It convinces you that some *thing* will make your journey richer; that without it, in fact, your journey will be incomplete. Discontentment, much like our overambition in Morocco, can lure you from a place of blessing without telling you the true costs involved. First Timothy 6:10 tells us that sometimes these costs involve the sacrifice of your relationship with God, the faith you once embraced, and your dearest relationships: "For the love of money is the root of all evil: which while some coveted after, they have erred from the faith, and pierced themselves through with many sorrows" (1 Timothy 6:10).

No one has any idea of the high cost of following discontentment at the beginning of the journey. Like us with our tour guide, we think we are in control of how much we will give up for what we want to get. But also like us with our tour guide, we may not be as in control as we think.

DEEPER THAN MONEY

If I were to ask you to name the top three reasons couples divorce, you likely would name financial disagreements as one of those. And statistically, you would be right. I have read that as high as fifty-seven percent of divorced couples cite money problems as a primary cause for their divorce.

But there has to be more to that statistic than meets the eye. It's easy to oversimplify statistics, and while there may be many factors involved in money-related marriage issues—including communication habits, transparency (or lack of it) in finances, expectations, and more—I would propose that disagreements regarding finances relate to an area we rarely consider in relation to marriage, contentment.

To be sure, contentment is larger than financial issues—far larger—and we'll look at some of these in this chapter. But because financial disagreements are a significant indicator of contentment, and because finances are so significant in marriage, we'll primarily look at contentment through the lens of finances. As we do, however, I'd encourage you to apply these truths to the larger picture.

BUYER BEWARE

Although the word *beware* only appears fourteen times in the New Testament, nine of these times, it comes from the lips of Christ Himself.

Jesus warned His followers to beware of false teachers, false doctrine, and the hypocrisy of the scribes and Pharisees—all cautions to which we would readily agree and often repeat.

But in Luke 12:15, Jesus used His *beware* to warn against a sin we easily excuse—covetousness. "And he said unto them, Take heed, and beware of covetousness: for a man's life consisteth not in the abundance of the things which he possesseth."

Covetousness—it's not a word we use very often. But it is a deceptive disease of the heart because it promises that something we don't have will make us happy. When we believe this lie, it will slowly consume our lives and relationships.

That promised *something* varies from one person to the next. Maybe your temptation toward discontentment comes in the area to which Christ was speaking in the verse above—possessions. Maybe you struggle with your financial status and wish you had more things, a more comfortable lifestyle, or more financial security.

Or maybe you wish for a different status in life. You long for recognition or affirmation. More online friends. More face-to-face friends. Deeper friendships. More opportunities. Greater respect.

Maybe you long for children that, for some reason, God hasn't given…at least not yet. Maybe you envy the way your friend's husband treats her. Maybe you wish your wife's appearance would change. Maybe you wish your husband's paycheck was larger or his career different. Maybe you would like your children to be more obedient or your home to be more comfortable.

Please don't misunderstand me. I'm not suggesting that it is wrong to try to better yourself or your life situation. If you long for children, pray for them. I have prayed with many couples to have children and have seen God answer in many cases—sometimes through surprise conception, sometimes through the discovery and treatment of medical needs, sometimes through adoption. Similarly, it is right and godly to provide for your family and pursue excellence in your career. There is nothing inherently wrong in reaching for something that you don't have through appropriate means.

But what is wrong is believing that *without* something you can't be happy. Whatever that *something* is for you— tangible or intangible—remember Jesus' words: "a man's life consisteth not in the abundance of the things which he possesseth." Your life and the story that God is writing is larger than a particular thing.

THE MEGAPHONE OF COVETOUSNESS

Covetousness has a broadcasting tool today that was unavailable in the first century—social media. It's not that social media is evil. I have it, use it, and am thankful for it. It's just that social media makes it fingertip easy to see all that we don't have and others do have.

After all, the fuel of covetousness is comparison. And social media makes it easy to compare.

Think about it this way: When does a wife most resent that her husband hasn't recently brought her "just because" flowers? Is it just when she is going about her day and is struck with the sudden desire for flowers? Or might it be when she sees her friends' posts about their "amazing husbands"? When does a husband most easily become frustrated with his job? Is it only in the moment when he's at work, and his boss is difficult? Or is it also when his friend is posting about his "perfect job" and how he is advancing quickly in his career?

Social media can touch deeper nerves of covetousness too. When you've had a fight with one another and parted ways with underlying stress, and then comes a private message from an old high school flame—"Hey, what's up? Saw you on here and wondered how you're doing?"—the discontent with your spouse already in your heart and the seeming innocence of the situation can make you more susceptible to making unwise decisions.

Does this sound over the top to you? I've seen too many couples in my office in gut-wrenching sobs over an affair that started online to so easily dismiss it.

Again, I don't think social media is evil. It's not. Anything sinful that comes of it is a result of sin in the heart, not from a screen. But social media does have a way of magnifying comparison and appealing to the covetousness that creeps into our hearts. And because it seems so benign and often has the illusion of secrecy, it has wounded many hearts and marriages.

If you use social media, I recommend shared passwords. (For that matter, if you use email, share your passwords.) Keep nothing hidden from one another. Even in your profile picture or description, make it clear that you are married and love your spouse. Talk about your spouse and your family positively. Have no suggestiveness or fishing back to old relationships.

Social media is *never* the place to complain about your spouse. Besides being a hurtful and wrong way to settle a disagreement or conflict, it makes your marriage more vulnerable to the advances of Satan.

When it comes to any online activity, remember that sin always thrives in secrecy. Your best defense is to keep everything about your life—whether it is physical or electronic—shared with your spouse.

HOW MUCH iS ENOUGH?

How much is enough? A survey conducted by *U.S. News & World Report* asked people how much money they would need to fulfill the American dream. Most people indicated they would need about twice what they already had.[1]

Our natural tendency is to think that more stuff equals a better life. We think if we can accumulate more things (material or intangible), we have come out ahead.

The apostle Paul, however, refuted this teaching in 1 Timothy 6. And after he did so, he defined for us what gain really is: "But godliness with contentment is great gain" (1 Timothy 6:6).

You see, coming out ahead in contentment is about more than doing without or being thankful for what you have. It isn't only avoiding a lifestyle of covetousness, but it is about embracing a lifestyle of godliness.

The real equation for blessing includes an eternal perspective.

Godliness + Contentment = Great Gain

Even if you could gain everything you wanted, you would discover in the process that you lost things you really needed—things like your relationship, your marriage, your walk with God, your testimony for your children. A covetous lifestyle is never satisfied but is always seeking more. A godly Christian who is finding satisfaction in Christ, however, will be content with the sufficiencies of life that God provides.

Hebrews 13:5 also speaks to the importance of a lifestyle of contentment: "Let your conversation [lifestyle] be without covetousness; and be content with such things as ye have: for he hath said, I will never leave thee, nor forsake thee."

How do we come to this place of satisfaction? What does the combination of godliness and contentment look like? What does a lifestyle of contentment + godliness look like?

Focus on the eternal over the temporal. Even the world knows that being content makes you happier. They know, as Benjamin Franklin so eloquently said, "Contentment makes poor men rich, discontent makes rich men poor."

But Christian contentment is more than just not wanting stuff. It includes valuing what lasts beyond this life.

If my heart is tangled around temporary possessions or desires, anything that stands in the way of these becomes an obstacle or a threat. For too many couples, that "anything" is even a spouse. And that is where much of the financial fighting comes into play.

But if my heart is focused toward the eternal, the whole game changes. Although I will deal with the necessary affairs of life and will provide for my family and do my best to be a steward of the temporal blessings God has entrusted to my care, these blessings won't consume my focus. When my heart is set on the eternal, it frees me from being entangled with the temporal.

This is exactly what God commands in Colossians 3:1–2: "If ye then be risen with Christ, seek those things which are above, where Christ sitteth on the right hand of God. Set your affection on things above, not on things on the earth."

Focusing on the eternal also allows you to lay up treasures in Heaven by giving to God's work. Jesus told us in Matthew 6:21, "For where your treasure is, there will your heart be also."

Trust in the Lord. Christian contentment not only frees me from false or fleeting loves, but it teaches me to trust in the Lord as my provider. A godly person learns to live in a trusting relationship with the Lord in every area of life, including the meeting of needs. Second Corinthians 5:7 reminds us, "For we walk by faith, not by sight."

Perhaps the best biblical example of this is the apostle Paul. As he thanked the church at Philippi for their generous gift of support for him and his work, he made sure to clarify that his ultimate dependence was on God: "Not that I speak in respect of want: for I have learned, in whatsoever state I am, therewith to be content. I know both how to be abased, and I know how to abound: every where and in all things I am instructed both to be full and to be hungry, both to abound and to suffer need. I can do all things through Christ which strengtheneth me" (Philippians 4:11–13).

Contentment, then, is not *self*-sufficiency (I have all I need); it is *Christ*-sufficiency (God will provide all I need).

Some of the sweetest times of drawing nearer to the Lord and to each other in our early marriage were during our times of greatest need. It was those circumstances when we had no money and empty cupboards that drew us to pray together. It was God's miraculous provisions that bolstered our faith together. These times enabled us to grow in our walk with the Lord and closer to one another like at no other times.

The world will tell you that trusting the Lord and focusing on the eternal are empty values. But then the world is full of fractured marriages, empty lives, and disappointment with unfulfilled dreams. Gain isn't everything; great gain is better.

BASIC PRINCIPLES OF STEWARDSHIP

When it comes to material or financial wealth, there are three basic principles that provide a foundation for contentment.

Ownership—*God owns everything.*

Psalm 24:1 says, "The earth is the LORD's, and the fulness thereof; the world, and they that dwell therein." Technically, I don't *own* anything, because everything that I have belongs to God.

Making a conscious decision to affirm this truth by "giving" everything I have to God helps me to better practice the next principle.

Stewardship—*God has entrusted me to manage assets for Him.*

What I do own from an earthly standpoint isn't mine to use as I see fit to advance my purposes. It is entrusted to me by God to manage for Him.

As stewards, all God asks of us is faithfulness—that we would manage the assets He has entrusted to us in the way that He would. After all, the determining characteristic of a manager's success isn't *volume;* it is *faithfulness.* This is why

1 Corinthians 4:2 says, "Moreover it is required in stewards, that a man be found faithful."

Provision—*God has promised to meet my needs.*

We have the freedom to be faithful with what God has entrusted to us because we have the promises of God that He will meet all of our needs.

Perhaps the greatest expression of trust in God's provision is giving. In fact, the strongest promises for provision in Scripture were first written to benevolent Christians. It was in acknowledging the sacrificial giving of the church at Philippi that Paul wrote, "But my God shall supply all your need according to his riches in glory by Christ Jesus" (Philippians 4:19). And it was in writing about the sacrificial giving of the Macedonian churches that Paul wrote, "And God is able to make all grace abound toward you; that ye, always having all sufficiency in all things, may abound to every good work" (2 Corinthians 9:8).

One of our favorite memories of God's provision in the early years of our marriage still brings tears to Terrie's eyes in remembering it. It took place about a year before we moved to Lancaster when I was still on staff at another church.

We had a small salary but had felt impressed of the Lord to give a large amount in a recent offering. A few

188 / ARE WE THERE YET?

weeks later, we found ourselves in dire need. It was Sunday afternoon, and I was supposed to leave that night to attend a pastors conference with the other men on staff. But, as Terrie informed me when we got home after the morning service, not only did we have no money, but we had no food in the house. I would be leaving her to go hungry.

We, of course, could have told someone our predicament, and they would have helped us. But that didn't seem right. Terrie's parents managed a Denny's restaurant, and they would have helped us as well. But I wasn't about to tell my in-laws that I couldn't provide for Terrie. Besides, her dad was not a Christian at the time, and we wanted to be a good testimony to him of the joy in serving the Lord.

I grabbed Terrie's hand and said, "Sweetheart, I only know one thing to do. Let's pray." In perhaps the only lapse of faith I ever remember in Terrie's life, she looked at me with tear-filled eyes and shook her head. I knelt while she stood, and began to pray.

I had no sooner begun presenting our need to the Lord than our phone rang. Terrie, who was still standing, answered it. On the other end of the line was Pastor Wally Davis, a dear man of God who is in Heaven now.

He explained that just that moment God had brought it to his mind that I had preached for his church about a month prior, but he had never given me a love offering. "If it's okay with you," he said, "I'd like to drive it over to your home this afternoon."

Less than an hour later, we were possessors of a one hundred dollar check—and a stronger faith.

FiVE HABiTS OF CONTENTED COUPLES

Let's take a closer look at the second principle—stewardship. After all, if we're going to manage what God has entrusted to us in a way that honors Him, we need to know how He would have us use it.

There are five basic habits taught in Scripture regarding finances:

1. Work—God blesses diligent labor, and work is the means by which He generally provides for our needs.

Proverbs 13:4 says, "The soul of the sluggard desireth, and hath nothing: but the soul of the diligent shall be made fat." Paul admonished the church at Thessalonica, "For even when we were with you, this we commanded you, that if any would not work, neither should he eat" (2 Thessalonians 3:10).

Biblically speaking, it is the husband's responsibility to provide for his family through labor. The Bible tells us that a man who doesn't provide for his family is an offense to the gospel: "But if any provide not for his own, and specially for those of his own house, he hath denied the faith, and is worse than an infidel" (1 Timothy 5:8).

I know that many couples have decided that in order to make it financially, both spouses need to work. Some women want to work because they enjoy a service aspect of their job. Some couples have chosen for both to work in order to meet some long-term savings goals. Ultimately, these types of decisions are between a husband and wife and the Lord. But from a pastoral counseling perspective, I would encourage you to as a couple get to the place where you do not *depend* on the wife's income as a long-term strategy for your family's needs. A wife should know that her husband will provide for her. And, as we have seen, provision is the husband's biblical responsibility.

Getting to this place may involve careful budgeting, paying off debt, downsizing, or even the husband changing his job or taking on a second job temporarily. It may also involve developing greater contentment.

2. Budget—Although a budget isn't mentioned in Scripture per se (although Jesus referenced a businessman's building budget as a basis for counting the cost of discipleship in Luke 14:28), living within your means is given by example throughout God's Word. A budget is a tool to be able to do this. Because the husband is to be the leader of the home and is responsible for the provision, it is wise for him to be the initiator of this process. But a budget should be something you both work out and come to agreement on together. For a budget to work, it has to be larger than paper or a computer screen. It has to be something you have both bought into and are committed to making work.

Part of living within your means includes avoiding debt. You may not be able to avoid it for larger purchases (such as a home), but don't get in the habit of living off your credit card. Not only will you regret it years down the road when you are using the money you could be enjoying in other ways to pay interest, but you will add a financial strain to your marriage that could be avoided. Proverbs 22:7 warns, "The rich ruleth over the poor, and the borrower is servant to the lender."

Through the years, Terrie has helped our family to live by a budget and avoid debt tremendously by her contentment and frugality. She has clipped coupons, learned to make more with less, and created fun family memories on a shoestring. Her willingness to partner in our family budget has drawn us closer to each other and helped us to work together for shared goals.

One of our favorite memories from our leaner years is our first anniversary. I was still in Bible college and we had no money, but I wanted to take Terrie to a nice restaurant. A little idealistically, I told her I'd take her anywhere she wanted to go, and then I held my breath.

"Let's go to Taco Bell," she responded. "And instead of just ordering a taco, let's each get whatever we want to eat."

We celebrated big that night. We got one of nearly everything off the menu.

3. Give—Giving really should come before budgeting because it should be the first item on your budget. The Bible tells us that the tithe, ten percent of your income, belongs to the Lord and should be given to Him first (Malachi 3:8–10; Proverbs 3:9–10).

But even beyond the tithe, God blesses generosity. Luke 6:38 promises, "Give, and it shall be given unto you; good measure, pressed down, and shaken together, and running over, shall men give into your bosom. For with the same measure that ye mete withal it shall be measured to you again." We discuss special offerings as a couple as well as commitments we make for weekly giving to missions and other special projects. I remember that the accountant who prepared our taxes in the early years of our marriage was surprised by our giving percentages, but we have enjoyed seeing God provide as we give.

Couples with a heart for the eternal see the material blessings of God not primarily as resources to increase their standard of *living*, but to be able to increase their standard of *giving*. The root word for *miserable* is *miser*. Those with miserly attitudes toward God often have similar attitudes toward one another. Giving to the work of God and to meet the needs of others is one of the most tangible ways we practice contentment.[2]

4. Enjoy—Sometimes talk of budgeting and giving makes people afraid they will have to live pinched, stingy lives. Actually, these practices free us to be able to enjoy what God has given to us without putting our trust in them. First Timothy 6:17 says, "Charge them that are rich in this world, that they be not highminded, nor trust in uncertain riches, but in the living God, who giveth us richly all things to enjoy."

Budgeting and avoiding debt allow you the freedom to enjoy the financial blessings of God without the weight of interest afterward. And using what God has given you to bless others allows you to enjoy your blessings doubled.

So go on a date night. Enjoy the provisions God has given you. Just bless Him for them as you do, and bless others with them as He enables you.

5. Save—As you make your budget and financial decisions, it is wise to remember the long view—retirement, provision for your wife should you die first, and an inheritance for your children. Proverbs 21:20 says, "There is treasure to be desired and oil in the dwelling of the wise; but a foolish man spendeth it up." Just because you have it now, doesn't mean you should spend it now.

I'm no financial guru, and I would certainly encourage you to read a good book, from a Christian author and perspective, on finances together as you create your financial plan. (Some authors of financial books I have read and been helped by are Larry Burkett, Dave Ramsey, and Randy Alcorn.)

But in all your financial planning, remember that the goal isn't to amass more wealth; it is to wisely steward your resources for the glory of God and the provision of your family.

ESCAPiNG THE TRAP

In his excellent book *Contentment,* Dr. Richard Swenson tells the story of a woman from New York City hosting a Russian visitor in the 1980s.

> They toured the Big Apple and saw the sights. The Russian visitor was unimpressed. "We have tall buildings in Moscow too…We have sports stadiums too." On it went: Russia has subways, parks, plays, concerts, the ballet. Finally, exhausted from touring, they headed home. The host quickly ran into a supermarket to pick up a few items. The Russian lady entered the store, froze in her tracks, and then started sobbing. Not even in her wildest dreams had she imagined thousands of different food items in one place.[3]

We become so accustomed to the gifts God has given us that we take them for granted. When we overlook the gracious provision God has already lavished on us, we search for significance and fulfillment outside the will of God, and we become prime targets for the tourist trap of covetousness.

So how do we escape the trap? How do we live with a heart of contentment?

The answer is simple: give thanks. "And let the peace of God rule in your hearts, to the which also ye are called in one body; and be ye thankful" (Colossians 3:15).

Giving thanks frees our hearts from the distraction of comparison. It protects us from the lure of covetousness. And it reminds us of the treasure we have in God and one another. Gratitude is the expression of a contented heart.

(above) Out for a stroll in Scotland

(left) With Danielle and Larry on Cayucos Beach—you can see the Morro Rock in the background

(above) The best moment of our day in Morocco

(left) Katie's most memorable moment in Morocco

NiNE

UNEXPECTED TURBULENCE

Trials

It was an early Monday morning in January, and we were finally leaving for a time of rest to celebrate thirty years of pastoring one church and thirty-six years of marriage.

That autumn had been incredibly full: Terrie's mom was in hospice care. Our grandson had been hospitalized and undergone serious surgery for the second time in less than six months. We had our annual church open house Sunday with weeks of intense outreach leading up to it. This was immediately followed by the shooting of a police sergeant known throughout our community. Our church was asked to conduct the funeral, which was a tremendous

198 / ARE WE THERE YET?

opportunity to minister to thousands of grieving officers. On the heels of this was Christmas outreach and then New Year's vision casting…. It just seemed like it had never stopped since early September. We were grateful to be on an airplane headed to Hawaii for some much-needed R&R that had been provided for and encouraged by our church family.

After our usual Sunday evening service, we had a late night with counseling and had only gotten a few hours of sleep before heading to Los Angeles International Airport. But all that was behind us now. We were on a Delta 757, hand in hand as the plane taxied away from the gate.

I rarely sleep on flights, especially 757s which are notably loud. The most rain we've had in Southern California in ten years was bearing down on us, and the pilot came on the intercom to tell us we were near a weather pattern known as Pineapple Express, which includes heavy wind and rain. He assured us, however, that we were ahead of the worst of the storm. Fatigue set in, and pretty soon, I had drifted off to sleep.

About an hour later, I jolted awake by a strong lean of the plane to our right. Strangely, at the same time, the plane seemed to be less noisy.

Sure enough, the captain came on the intercom again: "Ladies and gentlemen, you may have noticed we lost power of our right engine. We are working with ground maintenance and will be returning to Los Angeles."

Minutes after we turned around, the turbulence began as we flew into the storm we had been ahead of. I've experienced some rough turbulence in my days, but not in a 757 with one engine. I wondered what would happen if we were thrown by turbulence and couldn't recover because of having only that one engine. The man beside me had internet access and somehow found the maintenance record on the plane we were flying. He began to tell us of malfunctions dating as far back as 2004. Meanwhile, I wished he would pipe down. I could sense Terrie's blood pressure rising through her tightly clenched hand around mine, and my blood pressure may have been rising as well.

As we bumped along toward Los Angeles, the captain repeatedly came over the speaker. Each time, he said almost the same thing: "Ladies and gentlemen, I just want you to know that all is well. These planes often fly with just one engine. This is not uncommon." Again, "Ladies and gentlemen, once again, this is not unusual. We should land in about ninety minutes."

Eventually, I could see we were beginning to re-approach the airport. I knew that a pilot landing a 757 with two operating engines will normally reverse thrust from one engine to slow down on the runway. This time, however, we would be depending exclusively on the plane's brakes, and I couldn't remember if the man in the seat next to me had mentioned how recently they had been serviced. I prayed and watched out the window.

The sides of the runway were backed up with planes obviously told to clear to the side. Fire trucks with lights flashing were lined up by the dozens on both sides. *This is a lot of support for a routine landing,* I thought.

Thankfully, the landing was uneventful. We taxied directly to a gate (which *is* eventful at Los Angeles airport) and began to deplane.

As Terrie and I walked past the captain, I thanked him for getting us back safely. His response shocked me: "In my thirty-eight years of flying, that has never happened to me. We pilots experience it in flight simulators, but this was the first time in real life." And then he disappeared into the cockpit.

What? What about "This happens all the time. Everything will be okay. No need to worry"? It was nothing more than psychological comfort speech. It was helpful for a moment, but in reality, we all were flying through a first-time experience.

The next day, as Terrie and I sat reading, I thought again about the captain's words. Suddenly, it dawned on me: I serve a God who is the "Alpha and Omega, the beginning and the end" (Revelation 22:13). He is eternal in all His attributes, and He goes before me in every situation. When

He says, "Let not your heart be troubled" (John 14:1), He is not speaking as the God of simulators and hypothetical situations. He is speaking as the resurrected Saviour who is "touched with the feeling of our infirmities" and invites us to "come boldly unto the throne of grace, that we may obtain mercy, and find grace to help in time of need" (Hebrews 4:15–16).

When you hit turbulence in your life or in your marriage, you don't need to trust the counsel of others who have never been there or your own intuitions. You can trust the God who goes before you in every life storm to help you navigate as you rely on His Word.

TURBULENCE AHEAD

Nobody likes to anticipate turbulence—on planes or in life. Yet, if there is one thing we can be sure of, it is that we will face these times. Because every Christian couple goes through times of trial, we shouldn't be surprised by seasons of suffering. Addressed to Christians being persecuted for their faith, 1 Peter 4:12 says, "Beloved, think it not strange concerning the fiery trial which is to try you, as though some strange thing happened unto you."

And yet, it seems like suffering always takes us by surprise, doesn't it?

I remember reading years ago about the Waldensians who believed and preached the gospel in Italy during the twelfth century under the persecution of the Roman Catholic Church. I had always wanted to visit the valley where they lived. A few years ago, Terrie and I were able to do just that.

Our guide took us high into the Alps. It was breathtakingly gorgeous. But it was also steep, rugged, and dangerous. Deep into the mountains, our guide pulled up to a mountain hut. We got out of the vehicle and went inside. There we saw a plaque that read 'L Coulege Di Barba—The College of the Uncle. (The Waldensian pastors and teachers rejected the Catholic practice of calling spiritual leaders "father" because it contradicts the teachings of Christ. Instead, they called themselves "uncle.") This hut was a twelfth-century Bible college. And these mountains were where the followers of Peter Waldo hid as they continued to preach the gospel and carry on the Great Commission.

I was humbled as I saw the rough benches around the hewn stone podium where a "barba" would teach from the center. The eager students who attended these colleges were not only risking their lives in attending the school, but they were literally preparing themselves for martyrdom. When they graduated, they would become traveling evangelists who would preach the gospel message to an unfriendly audience. For many of them, it was not a question of *if* they would be martyred, but how much they could accomplish for Christ before they were killed by the Catholic Church.

Our guide then took us to a cave where Waldensians would gather in worship on Sundays, hidden from the view of those who would persecute them for preaching and teaching from God's Word. He told us the mountains were full of such caves and that many of them were used for either worship or hiding during this time period. This went on for over four hundred years as the Waldensian underground church continued to carry out the Great Commission of Christ in spite of tremendous persecution.

And then, in 1655, after a seeming lull to the persecution, the Duke of Savoy sent his army into the mountains and ordered a gruesome slaughter, referred to by historians as "the Massacre in Piedmont."

The horrors of this massacre are indescribable. Not content to simply kill their victims, the soldiers and monks who accompanied them invented barbaric tortures: Babies and children had their limbs ripped off their bodies by sheer strength. Parents were forced to watch their children tortured to death before they themselves were tortured and killed. Fathers were forced to wear the decapitated heads of their children as the fathers were marched to their death. Some of these Christians were literally plowed into their own fields. Some were flayed or burned alive.

Many endured worse. Unburied bodies—dead and alive—covered the ground. Hundreds of the Waldensians fled for a large cave in the towering Mount Castelluzzo. The murderous soldiers, however, found them there and hurled them down the precipice to their deaths.

As I heard this story and understood that even the few survivors of this massacre continued following Christ, I was deeply stirred. Right where we stood, Christians before us had stood for Christ, *knowing* it would mean persecution. Yet, they clung to God's Word, received His grace, and grew in faith. Their faith was a testimony to me that God's grace will be sufficient for *any* difficulty that comes into my life.

Although you may not be facing intense persecution as a couple, perhaps you are facing an incredible time of trial or pressure. You feel as though you are running from Satan's attacks, hiding in a cave of loneliness, watching destruction come in the lives of people you love, or facing any type of ongoing trial. Your trial may be financial—perhaps the loss of a job, trouble finding work, bills, debt, bankruptcy. Perhaps yours is health-related. Perhaps you're dealing with doctors, tests, treatment, hospitals, pain, exhaustion. Maybe your trial is a child who is struggling, rebelling, or has left the faith. Maybe you have lost a child or have not been able to have children. Maybe it is an unfaithful spouse, the death of your parents, a child with special needs, a deep life disappointment, a…. There are more possibilities than we can name here. But none of these possibilities surpass the grace of God.

These times of trial have the potential to make or break a marriage. On one hand, they can drive us to the Lord and to each other as we seek His help and recognize our need for His grace. On the other hand, we may respond wrongly to the trial and reject God's grace and allow the stress to drive us away from one another.

Think of Job and his wife. In one day, they lost it all—including their ten children. And then Job lost his health. We get a glimpse into the strain these losses placed on their marriage in his wife's first (and only) recorded words: "Dost thou still retain thine integrity? curse God, and die" (Job 2:9). Job's wife was allowing the trial to make her question God and even her husband's trust in God.

Job wisely responded, "Thou speakest as one of the foolish women speaketh. What? shall we receive good at the hand of God, and shall we not receive evil?" (Job 2:10).

Job persisted in trust, and it seems his wife came along as well. For at the end of the book of Job, God not only restored all that they had lost, but He also gave them ten more children.

God desires to bless you through your times of turbulence as well. Trials do place pressure on the most tender places of our hearts. But rather than allowing the trial to *destroy* your marriage, let God use it to *strengthen* your marriage. This happens when you together decide to respond to the trial in faith and trust.

READING THE INSTRUMENT PANEL CORRECTLY

One of our church members, Dave Wheaton, is a flight instructor and has occasionally flown me to meetings where I have preached. One of the first times he took me up, we encountered turbulence so great that I was thrown against the plane's frame, cutting my head. Through the entire flight, I noticed Dave's eyes were focused on the gauges.

Dave has impressed upon me the weighty importance of the instrument panel. He's explained how easy it is when you are enveloped in clouds to become disoriented regarding direction, altitude, and even whether you are right-side up or upside down. He's told me tragic stories of pilots who have crashed because when their intuition disagreed with the gauges in the cockpit, they trusted their intuition.

God's Word is to a Christian what the gauges of an instrument panel are to a pilot. The difference is that while a plane's gauges may get off or need to be recalibrated, God's Word never errs.

Often in times of life's turbulence, what we *feel* doesn't match what God's Word declares is truth. The temptation that comes to us during these times is the same as comes to a pilot when what he *sees* doesn't match up with what his gauges *say:* will we trust our intuition, or will we trust the reliable standard of truth?

Couples who trust their intuition respond like Job's wife. They look for the quickest way out of the suffering, rather than seeing God's purposes fulfilled through the suffering. They take stress out on each other. They lose hope. And many times, their marriages don't make it.

Couples who go through a trial while trusting in God's Word, however, find that even when their feelings are reeling, there is a center of truth on which they can stand.

When James, who was the pastor of the first-century church of Jerusalem, wrote to believers going through a time of severe difficulty, he challenged them to respond based on absolute truth, rather than on their changing emotions. He wrote, "My brethren, count it all joy when ye fall into divers temptations; Knowing this, that the trying of your faith worketh patience" (James 1:2–3).

If you are already familiar with this passage, you may have lost the shock of that first sentence. James literally says to consider your suffering as something that brings joy.

Joy?

Our natural reaction to trials is not joy. When a difficulty descends upon our lives, our reflex is usually worry, anxiety, perhaps anger. It is so easy in these moments to lose perspective of all that we know to be true from God's Word and to be filled with fear or frustration.

But this passage challenges us not to be an emotionally centered Christian, but to be a Christian who fully trusts in the truths of God's Word.

How in the world can we count our trials as joy?

First, it is by understanding the phrase *count it*. It comes from a Greek word used in financial accounting, *hegeomai*, which means "to deem, to consider." It is an admonition to step back to think about the bigger picture of what is happening and to trust that God is working through our trial in ways we cannot see.

I think back to this past summer when our three-year-old grandson, Chandler, was fighting severe, necrotizing pneumonia in the pediatric intensive care unit of a Los Angeles hospital. I remember sitting in the exact same waiting room and the exact same chair as I had just seven years earlier when our son Larry underwent major, intensive surgery as part of his treatment for cancer. And I remember, as I waited in that chair during Chandler's surgery, asking the Lord to help me not miss what He was trying to teach me in this experience.

There is no way I can fully describe all that God did in our lives this summer. But I can say that God worked in ways we never could have orchestrated. He taught us truths about His love, mercy, and faithfulness that, although they came from the pages of Scripture, we learned better in the weeks in the hospital than I had in weeks of study. He allowed us to minister to people—sharing His comfort and the truth of the gospel—whom we never would have met. And He taught us through the compassionate sacrifices of the nursing staff, doctors, and love of our church family and friends.

I won't pretend that we didn't struggle with fear during the process. We did. When I would see my grandson struggling for breath, when three nurses had to try inserting an IV seven times, when Chandler lay in bed with hot tears rolling down his cheeks, I struggled. During these moments of watching our grandson suffer, we had to choose to believe the truth of God's promises. In the midst of these fear-filled days, when we would reach out in faith for God's grace and believe, based on Romans 8:28, that He would work even this for our good and His glory, it brought peace to our hearts. In other words, we had to look at and trust the instrument panel of God's Word.

The apostle Paul learned how to accurately read the instrument panels. He had what he referred to as "a thorn in the flesh" (2 Corinthians 12:7). Paul never tells us what this was, but I believe it to have been a chronic physical difficulty of some kind, perhaps a disease in his eyes.[1]

It seems that for a time Paul was focused on the thorn, much like you and I tend to focus on our adverse circumstances. Three times Paul brought this matter to the

Lord in fervent prayer, pleading with God to deliver him from it.

But when the Lord answered Paul, it wasn't by taking away the thorn. It wasn't by taking Paul out of the storm. It was by refocusing Paul's vision on the instrument panel. Rather than granting healing, God assured him of sufficient grace: "And he said unto me, My grace is sufficient for thee: for my strength is made perfect in weakness." And what was Paul's response? He trusted the gauges rather than his feelings: "Most gladly therefore will I rather glory in my infirmities, that the power of Christ may rest upon me" (2 Corinthians 12:9).

During life's turbulence, we have two choices: we can trust our feelings, or we can trust God's Word. Our emotional instrument panels get off—sometimes way off. But God Himself never changes. You can trust that He is present, and He is working.

When you trust the gauges, it brings a renewal of joy.

WHAT DO YOU KNOW?

Another way that couples can learn to "count it all joy" during a time of suffering is to remember that we don't rejoice because of the trial itself, but because we know that God will work real benefits in our lives out of the trial.

The first two words after James' admonition to "count it all joy when ye fall into divers temptations" are *"Knowing this..."* (James 1:3). We don't rejoice because of what we are *experiencing,* but because of what we are *knowing.* What do we know that God will bring through trials? James 1 suggests three gifts God gives us in trials:

Confidence

Even when you already "know" God's promises in your mind, trials, like no other method, teach you what it means to have heart confidence in those promises. It is the very process of trials that allows us to *know* the truths we so desperately need.

Look at the first three words of one of the most familiar verses in all the Bible: *"And we know* that all things work together for good to them that love God, to them who are the called according to his purpose" (Romans 8:28).

We *know* this truth because it is written in God's Word. We know it because we see it in the lives of others in Scripture. But we know it in a personal way when we experience it in our own lives.

Endurance

God also uses trials to bring patience into our lives: "Knowing this, that the trying of your faith worketh *patience"* (James 1:3).

The word *patience* here is not just the patience of being able to wait for your appointment at the dentist's office. It means "steadfastness, endurance, perseverance." It is the patience that can be developed only over time.

This is the patience of a teenage football player in practice. He goes through drills and exercises and routines that leave him sore and achy and wanting to quit. But these very "pain-inducers" build muscle that he is thankful for when he is playing a real game.

Our problem is that we are so short-sighted we don't value patience. It's hard to be patient with an unruly toddler, a slow-in-coming test result, or spiritual growth in the heart of your spouse. It's not that we don't want God to work through trials—we do! But we don't understand that some of that work can happen only over time and behind the scenes.

Maturity

God desires to use trials in our lives to make us more like Jesus. Marriage itself is a picture of Christ and His love for us as His bride. In every trial we encounter as a married couple, God wants to bring us to spiritual maturity. We see this in James 1:4, "But let patience have her perfect work, that ye may be perfect and entire, wanting nothing."

The word *perfect* is from the Greek word *teleios*, and it means "finished, mature." Sometimes God uses the difficult chiseling of a trial to conform us to the image of Christ. Romans 8:28 is followed by verse 29, which tells us that the "good" God desires to bring out of the hard times in our lives is for us "to be conformed to the image of his Son."

I've seen this process of maturing in the lives of so many couples who have gone through trials together. As I write, there is a young couple from our church on their 175th day at the University of Los Angeles Medical Center where their baby Jackson is undergoing treatment for cancer. I've watched as Zack and Alaina have held each other and leaned into the Lord by the bedside of their son. I've seen them alternate sleeping nights and days, talking to doctors, getting meals, and finding ways to support one another as they take care of Jackson. And although I wish so much that Zack and Alaina did not have to endure the pain of watching their baby suffer, I have seen God strengthen and mature their faith through this trial.

This is what God promises in 1 Peter 5:10: "But the God of all grace, who hath called us unto his eternal glory by Christ Jesus, after that ye have suffered a while, make you perfect, stablish, strengthen, settle you."

HOLDING ONE ANOTHER IN THE STORM

One of the most amazing aspects of God's work in our lives through trials is that He can use a trial to strengthen the

Genesis 2 "weaving" process of melding two lives together. In an amazing tapestry of providence and grace, God can use these difficult times to weave two lives closer to one another, making their bond even stronger through a trial.

When our son Larry was diagnosed with cancer, he and Ashley had only been married two and a half years. I watched as Larry, in his sickest moments after surgeries and through chemo treatments, encouraged and reassured Ashley. I watched as Ashley was a picture of love and grace as she cared for Larry. Neither of them, when they exchanged vows at the wedding altar, envisioned these moments when Larry, with forty-two staples in his abdomen, was vomiting and Ashley was watching her husband suffer. Neither of them pictured wondering if they would be able to have children because of the effects of chemo. This wasn't really and truly what they had in their mind as they said "…in sickness and in health… to love and cherish…." But through these times, their walks with the Lord and their love for each other matured.

This kind of maturing, however, doesn't "just happen" as the natural outcome of a trial. Satan will do all he can to use a trial to weaken your relationship. He will try to bring confusion, hurt, isolation, misunderstanding, and doubt.

So what can you do to protect your marriage and grow closer to one another because of the trial? Walk through the trial *together*. Allow us to share five biblical and practical responses for enduring trials as a married couple.

1. Pray together. James 1:5 invites us to simply ask God for wisdom: "If any of you lack wisdom, let him ask of God, that giveth to all men liberally, and upbraideth not; and it shall be given him." As you go through a time of trial, there will be many decisions you don't know how to make, many needs you cannot meet. Ask God for His wisdom. As you do this together, He will draw your hearts closer to Him and to each other in prayer.

2. Trust together. Determine upfront that you will continue to trust the sovereignty and goodness of God. There will be many times when your hearts and minds are filled with questions. Take those questions to the Lord; but even before He brings clarity, trust Him. And trust Him together. One of the blessings of marriage is to encourage one another's faith.

3. Press together. I love the quote by Hudson Taylor, who was a pioneer missionary to China in the nineteenth century. Taylor himself was no stranger to trials, including burying his wife and five of his children in China. During one season of difficulty he wrote, "It doesn't matter how great the pressure is; what matters is where the pressure lies. See that it never comes between you and the Lord."

If this is true in our relationship with the Lord, it is also true in our relationship with our spouse. The trials of life bring a tremendous amount of pressure, and if that pressure wedges between a husband and wife, it can drive the marriage apart like almost no other force. But if that pressure instead pushes a couple closer to one another, it can strengthen their marriage like almost no other force. The difference lies in where the pressure lies.

We face pressure every day of our lives, but during times of difficulty, there is an added challenge in letting that pressure bring you closer to each other in that the normalcy of your lives is upset. It's hard to have a date night when your baby is in PICU, when your husband is temporarily stationed overseas, or when your wife is fighting a chronic illness. These are times to ask the Lord for wisdom, exercise creativity and flexibility, and allow the pressure to drive you toward each other.

4. Receive together. Through every trial of life, God offers us comfort. Second Corinthians 1:3–4 says He is the "God of all comfort, Who comforteth us in all our tribulation." Encourage one another to reach out and receive God's comfort. How does God give us His comfort? Through His Word, through the Holy Spirit, and through the local church.

Open the pages of God's Word, and receive His comfort. The psalmist wrote, "Unless thy law had been my delights, I should then have perished in mine affliction" (Psalm 119:92).

Allow the indwelling Holy Spirit to minister to your heart. Jesus promised His disciples, "And I will pray the Father, and he shall give you another Comforter, that he may abide with you for ever" (John 14:16).

And encourage one another to be faithful in church, even when you may want to withdraw. The entire book of James was written by the pastor of the church at Jerusalem. Through this letter, he reaches out with pastoral comfort to Christians spread throughout Asia Minor because of persecution. The local church is still one of the ways God brings comfort and care to His people.

5. Focus together. During a trial, there is a temptation to redirect the focus of the trial onto ourselves. Don't make the trial about you. Remember that it is ultimately about the glory of God. And along the way, focus on your spouse's needs, your child's needs, your loved one's needs—how God wants to use you to meet the needs of others. You have only so much energy to give. You can either direct your energy toward supporting and serving your spouse or toward sharing how difficult this is for you. If you will die to self and together focus on the other and serving those around you, God will bring great victories into your lives through the trial—and He will get the glory.

RIDING THE TURBULENCE

We were flying to Florida on budget tickets, separated from each other with rows in between us. I (Terrie) was disappointed not to be sitting next to my husband. I'm usually nervous about flying to start with, and I always appreciate the reassurance of being with him. To make matters worse, the lady sitting next to me didn't speak English, so we couldn't carry on much of a conversation besides smiling at each other.

Suddenly, we hit terrible turbulence. It was so bad that several passengers were vomiting as the captain came on the speaker to tell us he was going to have to land. My fellow passenger and I were terrified. Spontaneously, we reached for each other's hands and both started praying aloud—she in her language and I in English.

Aside from murmured prayers and occasional vomiting, the plane was quiet. I think we all thought we were going to die.

And then, just as the plane took another drop, a young child's voice from the front sang out, "Wheeeee!" He thought we were on a roller coaster ride. Every time, the plane pitched, he called it out again: "Wheeee!"

So was it turbulence or a roller coaster? It really depends on your perspective. To those of us whose perspective was shaped by fear, it was turbulence, and we thought we were about to die. To a little boy who had no reason to think the captain couldn't bring us through, it was an amusement park in the sky.

Through every storm of life, regardless of how gut-wrenching the turbulence becomes, you can trust your

Captain. He will bring fruit in your life through the trial. Until then, hold each other's hands and whisper, "Wheeee!"

After the turbulent flight, we had a wonderful time celebrating our anniversary in Hawaii

(top) A twelfth-century Bible college

(bottom) The mountains in Piedmont, Italy, where "the Massacre in Piedmont" took place

(top) Chandler in his early days of recovery

(middle) Twelve days after Larry's surgery, still with forty-two staples in his abdomen. Watching Larry and Ashley's spirit of faith and love for each other grow during these days was convicting and encouraging.

(bottom) Juneau, Alaska

TEN

SYNCING YOUR ITINERARIES

Busyness

Sometimes when pastors get together, they discuss hypothetical questions, such as, "If someone gave your church a million dollars that they won in the lottery, would you take it?"

Well, I can answer that question more than hypothetically. It wasn't a million dollars, but it was five hundred. And Laura, the would-be donor, presented it to me with an explanation: "I've been playing bingo for a long time, but I didn't start winning until I got saved!"

This is the kind of situation nobody teaches you about in Bible college.

The other thing nobody taught me in Bible college is what to do when a lady who cusses a lot wants to serve in ministry. Terrie had led Laura to Christ out of a rough background, and for Laura at age seventy-two, the sanctification process was slow. We created the "vacuum ministry" for her. It was a perfect fit, mostly because she could vacuum when the only people at church were church staff.

Laura is in Heaven now, but she loved our church and loved our family dearly. One time she came to Terrie and me to inform us that she wanted to send us on a vacation—"a real vacation." (We were a young couple who had been without a salary for sixteen months as we "restarted" Lancaster Baptist Church.) By this time, Laura had stopped gambling, so I didn't have to worry that she was giving us lottery money. Nevertheless, Terrie and I feel strongly that we are called to serve our church family and don't want to gain off of our relationships with them. I began to respond to Laura that we appreciated the offer but really weren't able to take a trip just then.

I can't print what Laura said next because it was the kind of words that opened her position in the vacuum ministry. After her mini rant, she explained, "You cannot do this to me. I already bought the tickets!"

And that is how Terrie and I ended up with tickets for a three-day cruise to the Bahamas.

Our flight from Los Angeles to Miami, where our cruise would begin, was a Sunday night red-eye. As usual, Sunday was a busy day full of teaching and preaching in our services and counseling appointments after church. By the time we had the kids settled with their babysitters and our luggage ready, it was late. We rushed to the airport and made it on our flight just in the nick of time.

As we flew over the Midwest, Terrie nudged me, "Do you have our cruise tickets?"

You know that awful feeling that comes over you when you forgot something important and it is too late to do anything about it? That's the way I felt just then. I knew right where the tickets were, too—on the kitchen counter, where I had set them out to not forget. There was no way we could get them before the ship's scheduled departure at 9:00 AM.

Thankfully, the cruise company allowed us to board using our driver's licenses as identification, providing that we were the last ones on the ship. But we spent a couple anxious hours wondering if we'd make it on and questioning how we could have been so foolish. Somehow, in all of the busyness of preparing for the trip, we had forgotten our tickets—the keys to open up the whole trip for us.

Sometimes we treat relationships like those cruise tickets. We acknowledge they are important, but we let

224 / ARE WE THERE YET?

them sit off to the side on the kitchen counter while we scramble to keep up with the more demanding aspects of our lives.

Our busy culture wars against real relational connection. With so many demands on our time, energy, and schedules, it's a challenge to give relationships the priority they deserve. And nowhere is this more true—or more dangerous—than in your marriage relationship.

When you are dating, it's comparatively easy to keep your relationship front and center. It's new, exciting, and consuming. But then you get married, and, well, it's not that your relationship feels less important to you; it's just that life has a way of shifting your focus. Children come, responsibilities change, urgent matters press. And somewhere along the line, busyness takes over. One day you realize that not only have you lost the points of connection you used to enjoy, but you also lost the oneness and emotional intimacy of your relationship.

WHERE THE FLOW LEADS

While on vacation at the family farm in Colorado several years ago, we went rafting down the Animas River near Durango. Before allowing us to rent the rafts and hire a guide, the rental company basically required us to sign our lives away: "I understand the risks involved and will not hold my guide responsible for dismemberment, loss of life, or...." I signed on the dotted line.

Once we reached the river, our guide continued the warnings. He explained that he would only be able to help us if we recognized that he was in charge and committed to follow his directions on our journey. Once on the raft, I easily understood why the guide warned and insisted that we let him be in charge. We could never have navigated those raging rapids by ourselves. And if we had chosen to just sit in a raft and "go with the flow," we surely would have capsized and drowned.

That guide knew where every turn, every rock, every branch, every change of current in the river was located. And, what's more, he knew how to guide inexperienced rafters through each place of danger.

The same is true in our marriages when it comes to our schedules and priorities. If we are not following the leadership of our Guide, the Holy Spirit, as He leads us to resist the natural currents of life, we will capsize and wreck relationally.

What happens in a marriage that just goes with the flow?

Emotional drift—If you are not regularly and purposefully connecting with one another, you'll drift apart emotionally. This is one of the reasons that Terrie and I carve out time weekly, usually over a meal, specifically

226 / **ARE WE THERE YET?**

for the purpose of hearing each other's burdens, syncing our schedules, and learning how to support each other in the process.

When a couple is dating, usually they hate being apart from one another; so even then, they are emotionally preparing to share the apart times with the other when they are reconnected. But if, as a married couple, you are not having times when you regularly connect and share with one another, over time, you'll stop thinking of one another when you're apart. Rather than going through your day with your spouse in mind, you'll disconnect emotionally and be more susceptible to the temptation to connect on a deep emotional level with someone else.

Build up of stress—The responsibilities of life bring enough stress on their own. But when you live with drifting priorities, the stress builds exponentially. And with these increased stresses is a tendency toward increased conflict with each other.

Neglect and resentment—When a husband neglects his wife because he is busy doing stuff, she usually will find replacements (children, volunteer activities, outings with friends, more hours at her job). But the cycle doesn't end there, because the husband then resents the extra stuff she is doing, thinking it is actually his *wife* who is neglecting *him*.

This cycle of neglect and resentment can start with either spouse. (In our marriage, it has usually started with me getting so wrapped up in ministry that I'm unintentionally neglecting Terrie.) But it won't end until both spouses step back, realign their priorities, and say, "You are more important to me than anything else in the world. How can I put you first?"

Remember that when God gave the operational definition of marriage in Genesis 2:24, He didn't say, "Therefore shall a man leave his father and his mother, and shall sometimes see his wife in passing…" or "and shall live under the same roof with his wife despite having varied schedules with nothing in common." He said, a man should "*cleave* unto his wife: and they shall be one flesh."

The word *cleave* means to "adhere…abide fast, follow close, overtake, pursue hard, stick." This takes intention. If you want to stay relationally and emotionally connected in the midst of a busy world, you will have to fight for it.

Usually what we want when it comes to synchronizing schedules is a life hack—a simple trick that makes it all work. But it has to start with determining what is important.

CLARIFY YOUR PRIORITIES

I've mentioned already that when Terrie and I travel, we do so a little bit differently from each other. But what I haven't mentioned is that when our whole family travels together, we do so *much* differently. At least, we go into it with different expectations. Our sons call the trip we took to England several years ago "The Forced March through England." To me, it was an awesome time of seeing places of historic significance to Baptists, religious freedom, and the Reformation. To our sons, it was a grueling "vacation" of going nonstop from 5:30 AM to 10:00 PM each day. (On the final day, they drew a line in the sand, stayed at the hotel, and played computer games while I visited one last museum.)

Don't get me wrong. I can do the whole "sleep in and rest until noon" vacation too. I just believe if you're going to do that, you may as well go to Cayucos instead of London.

In any case, it helps to be on the same page with everyone in your travel party about your vacation priorities before you leave.

The same is true in marriage. It isn't enough for you to independently define your priorities—you need to be in agreement on them.

When I plan my calendar, I do so by first identifying the key roles God has entrusted to me in life.[1] For instance, I am a Christian, husband, father, grandfather, pastor, Bible college president, friend, etc. Terrie's roles are a little different from mine. She isn't a college president, but she pours herself into the fourth grade Sunday school class she teaches, the ladies' ministry at church, and other roles. Our lists look something like this:

Paul's Roles	Terrie's Roles
Child of God	Child of God
Husband	Wife
Father	Mother
Grandfather	Grandmother
Pastor	Friend
Preacher/Teacher	Ladies Ministry Leader
Bible College President	Sunday School Teacher
Friend	College Instructor
Writer	Counselor
Mentor	Ladies Speaker

It is unrealistic to think that every activity of our lives would be shared; we simply have different responsibilities. What is important, however, is that the roles and priorities at the *top* of our lists are the same—and that we vigilantly guard these.

So what are your biblical priorities when you are married? The first is your relationship with the Lord, and the second is your relationship with your spouse. Every other priority must fall after these two.

Your relationship with the Lord—The primary priority for every Christian is his relationship with God. Deuteronomy 6:5 instructs, "And thou shalt love the LORD thy God with all thine heart, and with all thy soul, and with all thy might."

Remember that before God gave Adam a wife and the gift of marriage, God first established a relationship between Himself and Adam (Genesis 2:15–18). When our vertical relationship with God is not strong, our horizontal relationships with others will deteriorate.

In Colossians 3:9–10, God tells us to "put off the old man" and "put on the new man." To have healthy relationships with others, we must practice the exchanged life in which we put off the habits of our flesh and are renewed in our minds by God's Word to serve one another.

We must exchange self-will for a surrendered will to God.

> *That he no longer should live the rest of his time in the flesh to the lusts of men, but to the will of God.*—1 PETER 4:2

We must exchange fleshly desires for spiritual desires.

> *If ye then be risen with Christ, seek those things which are above, where Christ sitteth on the right hand of God. Set your affection on things above, not on things on the earth.*
> —COLOSSIANS 3:1–2

We must exchange human effort for spiritual power.

> *According as his divine power hath given unto us all things that pertain unto life and*

> *godliness, through the knowledge of him*
> *that hath called us to glory and virtue:*
> —2 PETER 1:3

These exchanges happen only as we personally seek the Lord and spend time with Him. This is why, just a few verses after this teaching on the exchange principle, Colossians 3:16 instructs, "Let the word of Christ dwell in you richly in all wisdom…." As God's Word fills our minds, we are then able to have the spiritual relationships described in the second half of the verse, "…teaching and admonishing one another in psalms and hymns and spiritual songs." When God's Word dwells in you, it changes you.

Through the ups and downs of every other realm of life, you must keep your personal walk with God as your top priority. As a Christian couple, you have the privilege of encouraging each other in this and also seeking God together. We'll return to this thought of shared growth in the Lord in our next chapter, so here I want to emphasize the importance of keeping your own heart tender to and seeking after God.

Perhaps the clearest biblical example of priorities is that of Mary and Martha, the sisters of Lazarus, who hosted Jesus in their home. While Martha was preoccupied with the responsibilities of entertaining company, Mary sat at

Jesus' feet, soaking in His teaching. When Martha chided Jesus for letting Mary sit while she hustled, He gently reprimanded her and gave her His focus concerning priorities: "And Jesus answered and said unto her, Martha, Martha, thou art careful and troubled about many things: But one thing is needful: and Mary hath chosen that good part, which shall not be taken away from her" (Luke 10:41–42).

One thing is needful.

There are many things that are important. But there is *one* thing that is needful, and that is your relationship with God.

One of our favorite places in the Holy Land was the Garden of Gethsemane where Jesus spent hours in prayer just before He was crucified, and apparently on other occasions as well (Luke 22:39). Part of what made this location so significant was its serenity. Near the garden was the busy and bustling city of Jerusalem. But inside, among the two thousand-year-old olive trees, was a place of solitude and peace.

This is what time spent alone with God in His Word and through prayer can be to your busy life…a refuge and a place of quiet where you can hear His voice.

You may wonder what this has to do with marriage. The answer is "everything." Becoming a better follower of Jesus also makes you a better husband or wife. A better parent. A better pastor. A better boss. A better employee. A better friend.

A real and passionate walk with the Lord, where you are growing in His Word and giving the Holy Spirit freedom to work in your life, will impact every relationship and aspect of your life.

And back to the matter at hand, you can't let the priority of your relationship with the Lord slide and expect that it won't affect your marriage. Keeping this relationship strong is needful even to your marriage.

Your relationship with your spouse—After your relationship with the Lord, the next priority is your relationship with your spouse.

Even over your children.

Even over your job.

Even over your ministry.

Although most people acknowledge that this is true on paper, many couples struggle to make this priority a reality amidst the demands of life. Along the way, husbands have a tendency to let their vocation supersede the priority of their marriage, and wives have the same tendency in letting their children supersede their marriage.

Early in our marriage, I was a knucklehead about this. Sometimes I would put so much energy into ministry that, without realizing it, I expected Terrie to just be happy with the leftovers of my time and attention. I'll be forever thankful for the wise, older pastor who observed this and told me, "Just remember, the church is Christ's bride, not yours. The church can get another pastor, but you can't get another wife."

This doesn't mean that you have to "guard your marriage from ministry" or, for that matter, from any line of work. In fact, some of Terrie's and my favorite things to do include serving our church family together. But what it *does* mean is that you have to determine in your heart that your marriage comes above your vocation or your ministry—that when you realize you're neglecting your marriage or your family, you're not going to just accept that as a "sacrifice" for the Lord or a sacrifice to further your career.

You have only so much time and energy. If something, even something that is a responsibility in your life, is going to do without some of that time or energy, it should not be your marriage.

If husbands have a tendency to put their vocation before their marriage, wives have a similar tendency to do the same with their children. Don't get me wrong. Our children and our grandchildren are the greatest treasures on earth. We will (and do) make any sacrifice necessary for them. But one of those sacrifices cannot be our marriage.

For one thing, the greatest gift you can give your child is to love your spouse. The security that this creates for your child is more valuable than any trade-off involved.

Second, the example you set for your children in making your marriage a priority will give them a pattern by which to build their future homes. All four of our children are grown, married, and raising their families. It is a joy to us to see our adult children put their relationship with their spouses first—including above their relationship with us. (And now that we've mentioned it, that's another implication of your spouse coming first. Once you're married, your marriage comes before your parents and in-laws. To *cleave* to one another, you are to *leave* your father and mother.)

Priorities do not set themselves. You must purposefully set them and then resist the natural drift away from them. This will include saying "no" to some opportunities or activities that don't contribute toward or that prohibit you from strengthening your relationship. But it is easier to say "no" to something when there is a greater "yes" burning inside. When you start by identifying your God-given priorities, it helps you identify that greater *yes*, making your needed *no* more clear.

SCHEDULE TIME TOGETHER

One of the best representations of your real priorities is your schedule. What we merely suggest we want to do "sometime" rarely happens, but what we actually schedule time for gets done. Just as a good financial manager will make a budget and first pay the mortgage and utilities before allotting money to eating out, so a conscientious spouse will designate quality time together before allowing their schedule to be filled with matters of lesser importance.

Think of this in terms of creating daily, weekly, and seasonal routines that draw you closer to each other. Yours may look different than ours, but here are a few suggestions:

Daily—Make it a priority during mealtimes to sit down with one another, set your phones aside, and talk. If you have children, this family mealtime won't be undivided attention for you and your spouse, but it is still vital.

Early evening, or just before bed, is another excellent time for connection. Give each other a minimum of fifteen minutes where you ask and listen and share about one another's day and pray together.

Weekly—Planning a weekly date night is, in my opinion, one of the most important habits you can set. This can sometimes be at home, provided you really do disconnect from the television, your phones, and independent projects. But go out sometimes as well. These dates don't need to be expensive, but they do need to be regular.

You need undistracted time to talk with one another. Again, this probably means setting your phone aside or turning it off. Try to pull away from the rest of the world for a while and just enjoy your spouse.

In addition to date nights, if you have children, you need to carve out undistracted family time. Once again, the idea isn't how much money you spend; it is how much time you spend. You can feed the ducks at the park, make ice cream sundaes at home, or read together as a family. Not only is this time important as a parent, but it also builds your marriage when you spend time together investing in your children.

Seasonally—Plan periodic times to get away with one another to focus on your marriage. This may be an annual couples' retreat, an out-of-town anniversary celebration, or a monthly "extra" activity with just the two of you.

I (Terrie) remember a time within the first few years of our marriage when my husband was so intently focused on ministry that I couldn't seem to get his attention. I mentioned once or twice that it would be good for us to plan some time together. But when that didn't work, I decided to take matters into my own hands, and I planned a surprise out-of-town getaway that I knew he would love. My goal was to create some time for just the two of us and to do it in such a way that would remind him how much he missed those times.

At the time, he was serving on staff at another church, so I clued the pastor in on my plans. I booked a motel room and lined up a babysitter. The day prior to my husband's weekly day off (which he had not been taking),

I offered to drive him to work so I could have the car for "errands." While he was at work, I packed our overnight bags, took Danielle to a babysitter, and then picked him up from work. When he got in the car and asked where Danielle was, I simply told him I had a surprise. It wasn't until we were on the interstate that I officially told him he had been kidnapped.

That little spontaneous getaway remains a special memory to us. We had a wonderful undistracted twenty-four hours together, and it proved to be a helpful reset for both of us.

LISTEN TO EACH OTHER

One of the most frequent questions I'm asked by young married couples going into, or newly in, ministry is, "How do you balance ministry and family?" The truth is, perfect balance is a myth. And that's not just for people in ministry; it is a reality of life.

Despite your best intentions, you will get out of balance in one or another area on a reasonably regular basis. That's because balance isn't static; it requires continual adjustments. Think of a tightrope walker constantly adjusting to keep his center of gravity on the rope. This is how life balance works as well.

The goal, then, is not to achieve "perfect balance," but to be willing to make adjustments along the way. It is obeying Galatians 5:25, "If we live in the Spirit, let us also walk in the Spirit." This requires that you remain sensitive to the Holy Spirit as He convicts you that you're not investing enough time in your marriage. But it also requires that you remain open and listen to any concerns that your spouse raises.

For us, this means we schedule time to pull out our calendars, evaluate how well we've been doing, discuss upcoming plans, and suggest needed adjustments.

I wasn't as good at this early in our marriage. Determined to be the "leader of the home," I wasn't particularly sensitive to concerns Terrie would raise about my schedule or about family time. (Hence, the kidnapping night she mentioned above.) While I am thankful for Terrie's patience with me and determination to keep creating times of making memories, I wish that I had been more understanding sooner. Even now, I sometimes have to slow myself down and intentionally create moments to listen to Terrie and ask her opinion on how well she feels we are syncing, and vice versa.

Seeing how much better we have gotten at this over time makes me thankful that we didn't give up trying years ago.

KEEP UP WiTH THE MAiNTENANCE

We—five pastors and our wives—were flying to Seoul, via a layover in Tokyo, to conduct a Spiritual Leadership Asia conference. It was a Saturday night in Tokyo, and I was scheduled to preach for Dr. Daniel Kim on Sunday morning.

As it came time to board the plane after our layover, it was evident that our flight would be delayed. That is always frustrating, but it's even more frustrating when the delay stretches out hour after hour, and you can't find anyone who speaks English who can tell you what is happening or how long the delay is expected to last.

As the clock ticked on past midnight, past 1:00, past 2:00, I became increasingly concerned that we would miss our preaching schedules for the start of the conference. But I still couldn't find any airline staff who could understand our predicament or explain what was happening.

Finally, at the last minute, an English-speaking manager appeared. He explained that the delay had been due to mechanical issues, which were now resolved and that the flight would begin boarding immediately. He even put all ten in our party in first class to thank us for our patience. We landed in Seoul at 6:00 AM and were preaching in churches throughout the city by 10:00.

But we almost missed that connection, simply because the plane wasn't prepared for flight. When it comes to your marriage, don't let the "mechanical issues" of failing to set priorities and schedule time with one another keep you from connecting.

We all believe in preventative maintenance for our cars. We know if we don't stop and change the oil every three to five thousand miles, our engine might blow. We rotate our tires and keep them balanced. And we take our cars in for periodic tune-ups.

So why not take time to pull over and sync your itineraries to avoid a marital blowup? Decide now that you will keep up with this kind of maintenance along the way. Don't let yourself get twenty or twenty-five years down the road with a successful career and retirement behind you and kids sent off to college—all of the things you've poured your life into, gone—and then you realize that your spouse is a stranger.

Ask yourself now, *What extra thing in my schedule could be set aside to improve our time for relational development?* Invest the time now in syncing your itineraries so you can enjoy the journey *together*.

(top left) At the ancient fortress of Megiddo in northern Israel

(top right) On the cruise from Laura—we were just thankful we made it

(left) During one of the calmer moments of our rafting trip in Colorado

(left) Walking to visit Spurgeon's grave during "The Forced March through England"

(middle) The olive trees in Gethsemane are two thousand years old, possibly the same trees Jesus prayed near just before Calvary.

(right) The Garden Tomb is a sacred place of many for the world's greatest miracle.

ELEVEN
BECOMING A WORLD-CLASS TRAVELER
Growth

If you go to the Valley of Elah in Israel, you can easily envision the events of 1 Samuel 17. Along the slopes of the south side, the Philistines gathered, and along the north side, the Israelites gathered. There in the middle is a triangular-shaped valley where David defeated Goliath.

The Valley of Elah is a great place to visit because, unlike so many of the biblical sites in the Holy Land, this location doesn't have a more modern structure built on it. It is still open, rugged, empty—just as it was when David overtook Goliath with stones from the brook that still runs through the valley.

In fact, the valley is full of stones—something that caught our attention when our family visited. I don't remember whose idea it was first, but we started thinking about how much we would like to bring some of those stones back to the States. I thought of our thirty-five deacons and pictured mounting a stone on a plaque to give each one. Then I thought of a new ministry project the Lord had been laying on my heart and thought I'd like to give a similar plaque to those who partnered with us in it. Terrie thought of her Sunday school class of thirty or forty girls. She thought she'd like to give each of them *five* stones from the Valley of Elah.

The more we thought about how useful the rocks could be and who would enjoy having them, the longer our list grew. Suffice it to say, we left the Valley of Elah with a few hundred stones. Fortunately, there were enough of us that we were able to come up with enough bags or backpacks to carry our rocks out and leave them on the bus for the rest of the day.

It wasn't until we were packing to leave the country a few days later that we began to have misgivings about our rocks. Are you allowed to carry rocks out of Israel? Or is it like the national parks here in the States where you must leave it all just as you found it? Also, Israeli airport security is thorough. Even if taking rocks is no problem, does having a few *hundred* rocks in your baggage seem suspect? And finally, although we brought small rocks, collectively, they were still quite heavy.

Our solution was to divide the stones throughout the luggage in our group. Only one bag ended up having a large concentration of rocks, so we felt secure as we left.

When you travel internationally, you usually are allotted two suitcases for your luggage. Not everyone in our group needed two suitcases, and some wanted to bring more (Terrie brought two suitcases of just snacks for all of us), so it all evened out. But it did mean that each person needed to take two bags through security.

Our daughter Kristine had her bag and took another bag from Terrie. As she went through security, her suitcase was one of the many to be randomly selected for personal inspection. As the security agent pulled the bag off the conveyer and motioned for Kristine to step aside, Terrie and I realized our mistake at the same time. Kristine didn't know that she got the bag full of rocks.

As the agent began to open the bag, he asked Kristine a series of questions: "Is this your luggage?"

"Yes."

"What is inside?"

Kristine knew better than to say she didn't know what was in the suitcase, because that would make it look like she had agreed to carry luggage for a stranger. So, she demurred, answering slowly with filler words as the security agent began opening the bag.

"Weeelll," she drew out, trying to catch a glimpse of what was inside as he opened it. "There's some…" and just then she caught that hoped-for glimpse, *"Rocks?!"*

Needless to say, the security agent had a few more questions.

Travel is full of the unexpected. But the longer you travel, the better you adapt to issues as they arrive. You become more experienced and you grow as a traveler. You learn to carry fewer rocks and how better to divide them along the way.

Unfortunately, the same is not always true in marriage. All too often, we talk with couples who have been married fifteen, twenty-five, thirty years, but rather than developing as a couple, they have stagnated. Instead of getting further along, they've fallen into ruts of hurtful relational habits. Rather than growing closer to one another, they become distant or even hostile.

How does this happen?

Actually, a better question is, *How can we keep this from happening to us?* After all, growth isn't automatic. It isn't merely by being married for a decade that you become a better spouse; it is by intentionally pursuing growth.

THE iNTERTWiNiNG OF TWO LiVES

This week, a photo of a couple having a date night at Wendy's went viral. With nearly thirty thousand shares and five thousand comments on Facebook, this picture clearly captured people's attention.

You might guess that for this kind of reaction the picture was of a famous couple—perhaps Hollywood celebrities on their fourth marriage. Or maybe it was a couple discovering bad customer service or improper food handling at Wendy's. After all, fame and negativity are two things that spread well on social media.

The picture is better than either of those. It is of an elderly man feeding his wife. They are sitting next to each other, but on either side of the corner of the table. She has her eyes closed; he has his hand by her mouth as if he has just put in a fry. A tray with an empty fries box, a drink, and sauce is in front of them.

Another customer took the picture and posted it on Facebook. She described noticing them together and wishing she could experience a love that strong. She wrote,

> The gentleman got up from his seat to throw his food away and I couldn't resist asking how long he and his wife had been married. He looked at me and asked me to guess his age but not to guess too low. After a few guesses he told me he was ninety-six and his wife

> is ninety-three who is suffering from Alzheimer's. This is their date night. He also told me that if they make it till June, they will be celebrating seventy-five years of marriage!
>
> Getting all the way to the end of the line with the person you started out with is one of the most glorious things on the face of this earth. Could a couple be more blessed than to have that happen? To share a deep love and bond that only grows as we age, that is a beautiful thing.[1]

Seventy-five years and still having date nights. How does a couple keep their love strong over the challenges of time and disease and need and stress and the difficulties of life?

As we have already seen, God designed for marriage to be more than an "okay relationship" where each person has their own agenda and appreciates the other on an as-needed basis. Marriage is to be the weaving together of two lives: "Therefore shall a man leave his father and his mother, and shall cleave unto his wife: and they shall be one flesh" (Genesis 2:24).

This kind of weaving takes both time and effort. Over the years, provided you continue investing effort, you build a repository of shared experience that draws you closer to one another. As you intentionally lean in to each other through every phase of life and share together in the decisions, plans, events, and memories, you grow closer. And as you, through this process, give attention and intention to your relationship, you become a better spouse as well.

In this chapter, let's look at five specific ways you can pursue this kind of growth.

GROW TOGETHER IN CHRIST

Only growth in grace can give you the desire and ability to unselfishly invest in your marriage. So determine that you will be a couple who grows in grace *together.* First Peter 3:7 instructs, "Likewise, ye husbands, dwell with them according to knowledge, giving honour unto the wife, as unto the weaker vessel, *and as being heirs together of the grace of life;* that your prayers be not hindered."

Notice that phrase "as heirs together of the grace of life." When you are heir to something, it isn't yours unless you avail yourself of it. If I found out tomorrow that I had a long-lost relative who had left me with a multi-million-dollar fortune, that money would only influence my life as I used or invested it. An inheritance that simply *exists* doesn't help anyone. The same is true of growing in God's grace. Through salvation, we have access to the very throne of grace, but even there, God encourages us to ask for grace (Hebrews 4:16).

How do you avail yourself of the grace of God? We already saw in chapter 2 that it requires humility (James 4:6). But it also requires that you reach for it using the means God has provided to give us grace—prayer, His Word, biblical preaching, serving others, and other spiritual disciplines that God's Word calls us to practice. The same passage that tells us God gives grace to the humble also instructs us, "Draw nigh to God, and he will draw nigh to you…" (James 4:8). Part of the way we draw near to God is through these spiritual disciplines.

As you pray together, have family devotions, attend church, learn to tithe and give, dedicate your children to the Lord, serve in your church, hold to God's promises, rejoice in His answers to prayer…as you do these things together, over time your hearts intertwine with one another in shared grace.

The trend in our culture—even some church cultures—however, is to practice these things *less*. There are people who will tell you to put your marriage before your relationship with Christ and that to pursue growth in grace through spiritual disciplines is legalistic. They'll tell you that if you need Sunday morning for a date time, it's more productive for your marriage to skip church. If you are experiencing financial strain, you should stop tithing. If serving makes you tired, you should stop. In a nutshell, they'll tell you that your greatest problem is that your life is too full and that to simplify, you should cut back on everything that doesn't bear immediate results.

There are many aspects of this thinking that are unbiblical. One of them is that God calls us to put our relationship with Him before any other relationship or goal of life and that discipleship that is worth something costs something (Matthew 10:37, 22:37). But in relation to what we are looking at in this chapter, the idea that you should be less active in pursuing Christian growth is simply shortsighted. Yes, perhaps if you do not tithe on a particular week, it will ease your budget. Perhaps if you sleep in on a Sunday morning, you'll feel more rested that day. But that is a shortsighted way of looking at life and it dismisses the impact of growth over time. It is these very means of growth in grace that actually strengthen your marriage and draw you closer to one another.

You don't want *less* growth; you want *more*. Rather than pulling back from the spiritual activities that help you grow as a couple and as a family, work to increasingly make them part of the daily and weekly routines of your life.

CREATE TRADITIONS AND MEMORIES

Traditions are so healthy for a relationship. They tie your past to your present and help you look forward to the future.

Terrie is an expert at making traditions special and purposefully creating memories along the way. She has done this for the two of us and also for our entire family. Over the years, she has been one to make each child's birthday special, decorate the house with each change of season or holiday, create moments for memories (and remind me to slow down long enough to enjoy them), and develop traditions.

As a family, some of our most cherished memories are of summer vacations, usually at the family farm in Colorado. For years, we made the eleven-hour drive to spend vacation time with my grandparents out on the family farm. For us, it was a budget vacation and a great way to get time away. The open expanses of farmland surrounded by rugged mountains has always felt restoring and renewing to me. For our kids, it was exciting to be out on the farm, hiking the canyon and its rock ledges, and fly fishing with great-granddad.

Other family traditions have been Terrie making gingerbread houses with the kids (and now the grandkids) at Christmas time, me setting up the train around the Christmas tree in our living room with the boys (and now grandsons), attending our boys' basketball games and our girls' cheerleading. Another tradition got created because of a schedule conflict. Our daughter Kristine's birthday is in October, and it always seemed to fall on the week of our church's annual missions conference when we were hosting missionaries in our home. As Terrie and I thought about it, we didn't want Kristine to feel cheated out of a birthday celebration, so we decided to make it a *big* celebration, including the missionaries in it. I don't think Kristine really believed us when we told her the missionaries came just to celebrate her birthday, but she did grow up with a heart tender toward missions.

Our single favorite vacation memory with our family, when our kids were teenagers, was a vacation to Hawaii where we met a young man named Todd, a student at Colorado State University, who was working in a Thomas Kinkade shop. Terrie and I were looking at a painting, and I spoke to him about the fact that we like Kinkade paintings because he included John 3:16 at the bottom of every one. Todd asked what the verse said. (He had seen the reference at CSU basketball games where he played but had never heard the verse.) We sat down in the showroom, and God gave us twenty minutes of uninterrupted time to share the gospel with Todd, who accepted Christ as Saviour. Todd joined us that night for dinner and every night thereafter, and we had the opportunity as a family to disciple him.

These kinds of memories have a way of knitting your hearts together as a couple and as a family. It has always been interesting to me that the kids say this was their best vacation—not because of the experience they enjoyed, but because of watching another soul come to Christ.

As a couple, one of our regular traditions is to read a book on marriage each year either before or during the time we get away to celebrate our anniversary, and to talk about it during that time. Our anniversary falls the week between Christmas and New Year's, so we almost never leave on the day of our anniversary. (This week is full on our calendar because of the Christmas programs leading up to it and then preparing for a first of the year vision casting service for our church immediately after.) While we have a nice meal on our actual anniversary, we look forward to the tradition of spending a few days together in January to enjoy one another and focus on building our marriage.

I am so thankful for the many ways God has used Terrie in my life. And her ability to make memories special is right there near the top of the list. She is the one who has, over the years, nudged me to remember the importance of making room for memories by weaving tradition into our lives. As I look back over the years, I see how instrumental these traditions have been in creating the strength of the fabric of our family.

LEARN FROM YOUR MISTAKES

If there is one way to grow in any area of life, it is learning from your mistakes. This is good news because most of us have plenty of raw material from which to draw, especially when it comes to marriage.

Learning from your mistakes doesn't necessarily mean you'll never make the same mistake twice (I wish!), but it does mean that you will draw wisdom from them and grow. Proverbs 15:31 says, "The ear that heareth the reproof of life abideth among the wise." When you do something that doesn't work out, analyze why, and make adjustments going forward.

One year when our kids were still young and we were going to drive to Colorado for our summer vacation, I told everyone the day before that we were going to leave at 6:00 in the morning. I had worked out in my mind the sequence of cities we would drive through and what time we'd be at each—Barstow by 7:30, Needles by 9:30 or 10:00, Kingman by 11:00 and Flagstaff for lunch. From there we'd be good for the rest of the afternoon and arrive at the farm by 6:00 PM.

Somehow, we all slept in that morning; we were supposed to leave and didn't even wake up until 8:00 or 9:00. So before we even got on the road, I was frustrated and more than a little edgy. Terrie had already packed, so while everyone else got dressed, I grabbed the suitcases and threw them into our Mitsubishi Colt hatchback wagon. When the kids were ready, I threw them in too.

Somewhere around Needles, California, I asked Terrie for my sunglasses. She told me they were in our blue suitcase, so I asked our son Larry to reach into the back and get my sunglasses. After a few moments of hanging over the back seat and digging among the luggage, Larry reported that there was no blue suitcase.

"Which blue suitcase are they in?" I asked Terrie.

"The one I told you to get from the top of the stairs as we were leaving."

"Oh, *that* blue suitcase."

In the frustration and hurry of the morning, I hadn't really paid attention. I did end up paying money though. The blue suitcase held all of Terrie's and my clothes and toiletries. We had to stop in Flagstaff to replace all the essentials that were in the suitcase still sitting at the top of the stairs.

I wanted to blame Terrie for the mistake. Why didn't she check to make sure it was in the car? Why didn't she notice that I hadn't heard?

But if you blame each other for your mistakes rather than learning from them, the mistakes cost you double— the original discomfort and then whatever it costs to keep having the issue circle until you finally learn.

I'm not saying I've never failed to listen to Terrie since or that I've never gotten frustrated with delays again, but

I can say that I took the lesson to heart and have invested more effort in listening instead of rushing.

GET HELP AS NEEDED

Before we got married, we committed to one another that if either of us ever felt we would benefit by getting marriage counseling, we would both do it.

And, in fact, there did come a time in our lives when our ministry was growing so rapidly that I was investing more and more time in the church, and Terrie began feeling neglected. It was frustrating to both of us because our heart really was that we both wanted to see the church grow, and we both wanted a strong marriage. We just didn't know how much of this sense of tension between the two desires was normal—if it was just a short-term phase, or if it needed adjustment.

The concern persisted for Terrie, however, and so together we sought counsel from a pastor who was twenty years further in ministry to help us discern what was going on. One of the things he told us was what I mentioned in the previous chapter about the church being Christ's bride not mine. So, yeah, basically he told us Terrie was right.

Looking back, I'm so thankful we followed through on our commitment to seek help, even though, at the time, I really thought we were doing fine. The counsel we received then marked a turning point in my thinking, as that pastor helped me understand the importance and irreplaceability of my role as a husband and father.

I tell you this because sometimes couples think of marriage counseling as a last resort and that, even by going, they are saying that their marriage is on the rocks. The book of Proverbs, however, teaches us that one of the ways we get wisdom in life is by seeking counsel.

> *Where no counsel is, the people fall: but in the multitude of counsellors there is safety.*
> —PROVERBS 11:14

> *The way of a fool is right in his own eyes: but he that hearkeneth unto counsel is wise.*—PROVERBS 12:15

> *Without counsel purposes are disappointed: but in the multitude of counsellors they are established.*—PROVERBS 15:22

> *Hear counsel, and receive instruction, that thou mayest be wise in thy latter end.*
> —PROVERBS 19:20

> *Counsel in the heart of man is like deep water; but a man of understanding will draw it out.*—PROVERBS 20:5

For by wise counsel thou shalt make thy war: and in multitude of counsellors there is safety.—PROVERBS 24:6

Seeking counsel doesn't need to be a last resort. It can be simply one of several tools to provide maintenance along the way.

There are a few important things to understand, however, before you seek counsel: first, talking about your spouse to others is not the same as getting counsel. If you tell you parents, coworkers, or friends (even Christian friends by way of a "prayer request") about something you perceive to be a weakness in your spouse's life, your spouse will feel betrayed, and you will actually make the situation worse. If you are looking for help solely with your responses and not with trying to change your spouse, go to someone who has at least two decades more experience in marriage than you, and share nothing that you wouldn't share if your spouse were present.

Second, you want counsel that comes from a biblical perspective. If you ask secular counselors for help, he or she may be able to give some common sense advice, but they will not have the insight that comes through a thorough understanding of biblical truth. And worse, their advice is likely to be humanistic, focusing on making yourself happy, even at the expense of your marriage. The kind of advice that you really want is gospelistic—focusing on God's grace, sacrificial love, and the covenant of marriage.

Finally, the most helpful counsel is not going to come from your peers. Going to couples who are in a similar life stage as you for help can, in fact, be detrimental. In most cases, they simply do not have the perspective of time and experience to help you. For example, if Terrie and I had gone to another young pastor who was in the early stages of building a ministry and asked him to help us grow in our marriage, he wouldn't have known much more than we did. He would have been in more or less a position to basically take sides (was Terrie right or was I right?) rather than to help us discern the heart of the matter and which biblical principles we needed to apply. When you sense you may need help, I would challenge you to go to a spiritual leader (such as your pastor) or a couple who is more mature in the Lord and has been married a couple decades or more longer than you.

As a husband who has needed counsel and as a pastor who has often been asked to give counsel, allow me to share four ways you will gain the most from counsel.

1. **Go with a humble spirit.** Even if you are not the spouse who desired a counseling appointment, go into it with a teachable, humble spirit. Don't go with an attitude to prove you are right and your spouse is being overly

sensitive or misunderstanding. Ask the Lord to give the counselor wisdom and insight and be willing to share openly, honestly, and humbly. First Peter 5:5 says, "Likewise, ye younger, submit yourselves unto the elder. Yea, all of you be subject one to another, and be clothed with humility: for God resisteth the proud, and giveth grace to the humble."

2. Be prepared to take notes. Proverbs 19:20 instructs, "Hear counsel, and receive instruction…." But I'm amazed at how often people come for counsel with no notepad or pen or indication they intend to take any notes at all. Sometimes it is not until I suggest they may want to write something down, that they pull out their phone to type or ask for paper. If you go to someone for counsel and are hoping to learn, be prepared to record what you are given so you can review, think on, and evaluate how well you are implementing it later.

3. Follow through on assignments. Most counselors will give you an assignment, perhaps a project or reading, that relates to truths they shared with you and needs that were unsurfaced in your meeting. Take seriously any assignment you are given, and invest the time necessary to follow through on it. To ask for counsel but not accept the responsibility to pursue growth is a waste of your time and the counselor's time. Change doesn't happen simply because you *hear* truth, but because you *respond* to truth.

262 / ARE WE THERE YET?

James 1:22 says, "But be ye doers of the word, and not hearers only, deceiving your own selves."

4. Set up accountability. When you see a need for growth or change in your life through counseling, set up checkpoints with the person or couple you have gone to for counsel to evaluate growth and ask further questions that have come up. Don't look at counseling as the *end* of your help, but as the *beginning* of it. (The continued availability for ongoing accountability is another reason it is good to ask your pastor or a more spiritually mature couple in your church for counsel.)

TRUST GOD TOGETHER

On the same trip that Kristine brought home a suitcase of rocks for us, her husband Jon's suitcase was lost. When they arrived back in Los Angeles, his suitcase was simply nowhere to be found. They tried calling back to Tel Aviv to ask if it could have gotten on another flight. It was Friday evening in the United States, which meant it was Saturday—the Sabbath—in Israel, and no one could help.

Next, Jon and Kristine tried calling the travel agency through which we had booked the flight. Their records showed that the suitcase had been with us on our flight and should be even right that moment on the luggage carousel.

For weeks, Jon and Kristine filled out forms, made follow-up calls, filled out more forms, waited, made more calls…. About six months later, they gave up and figured the suitcase was long gone.

Not long after they reached this conclusion, Jon received an incoming call on his cell phone from a number he didn't recognize. He answered, and the man on the other end asked for "Jon Sigh-son." (Their last name, Sisson, is pronounced "Sis-son.") The odd pronunciation was a clue they hadn't met before. But, Jon's luggage had met the caller.

In a strange twist of events, this man had recently lost his luggage and reported it to the airline. When they sent it to him, it turned out to be Jon's missing suitcase. Two days later, the bag was delivered to Jon and Kristine's front porch.

Like travel, sometimes life and marriage are unpredictable. Although experience does make you better able to adapt to the unexpected, it can't change circumstances beyond your control (including lost luggage).

This is where faith comes in. Faith isn't refusing to invest yourself and just hoping it all comes together. Faith is pursuing growth, making adjustments, and trusting that through all of that, God will weave your lives together for His glory.

Hebrews 11:6 tells us, "But without faith it is impossible to please him: for he that cometh to God must believe that he is, and that he is a rewarder of them that diligently seek him." Faith is what assures you that your diligence will be rewarded by God Himself.

So yes, you grow together in Christ, create traditions and memories, learn from your mistakes, and get help from others…but ultimately, you recognize that you're not fully in control. God is.

Continue diligently investing in the process of growth. But do it with a heart of faith in God's promise to reward your efforts.

The village of Capernaum is on the northern side of the Sea of Galilee and was Jesus' base during much of His Galilean ministry

At the farm in Colorado, cutting a Christmas tree with Matt and two of our granddaughters

With a Palestinian shepherd in Elah

Colorado, 1989

Colorado, 2015

TWELVE

ADVENTURE AWAiTS

Purpose

Without a doubt, the most adventurous road trip Terrie and I have taken together took place several years ago in the country of Nicaragua. I had been invited to the country to preach in churches that were planted by a veteran missionary and to do consultation regarding starting a Bible college for Nicaraguan pastors. Because of the renowned instability of Nicaragua, our church deacons strongly recommended that we bring with us two men from our church who are experienced police officers with a background in military reconnaissance.

We spent the morning of that adventure-fated day distributing food to residents who lived just outside the citywide garbage dump on the outskirts of Managua, and then visiting a church located about five hundred yards from that dump. The sacrificial service of the pastor and his wife at this church was humbling and challenging to us. We couldn't help but think of Jesus' example in 2 Corinthians 8:9, "For ye know the grace of our Lord Jesus Christ, that, though he was rich, yet for your sakes he became poor, that ye through his poverty might be rich."

From Managua, we headed into the mountains to the city of Matagalpa. We (another pastor, Terrie, me, and the two police officers from our church) traveled in a van with a hired driver about fifty yards behind a lead car. As we approached a bridge spanning the Rio Grande de Matagalpa (the second largest river in the country), the lead car radioed that we should hold our position because there was trouble on the bridge.

Apparently, the Sandinista guerrillas (representing the socialist party of Nicaragua) were on some form of strike or making a political statement of some kind. The reason was lost on us, but the fact that they had completely blocked the bridge and were demanding extortion payments for anyone wanting to cross was not. Even from our position fifty yards back, we could see hundreds of soldiers carrying Russian-made semi automatic rifles. They had strips of bullets strapped across their chests and were shouting in Spanish.

Because of the reputation Central American countries have for kidnapping foreigners, the police officers who were accompanying us had an immediate uneasy feeling about our situation. Terrie's feeling was much worse.

Suddenly, from out of nowhere, a man dressed completely in black from head to toe appeared by the side of our van on a motorcycle and said, "If you want to have some safety, I know a shortcut. Pay me and follow me." He spoke in Spanish. One of the police officers with us translated. The man on the motorcycle and our driver continued to talk back and forth in Spanish, as we strained to pick up any words we recognized, and the police officer with us kept telling the driver that this was not a good idea. Before we knew it, our hired driver made a sharp turn to the left, and we were following a guy on a motorcycle, who none of us knew but who had just taken money from us, down a dirt road into the rainforest—really, the perfect place for kidnapping people.

About four miles into the rainforest, he took a turn to the right and headed back toward the river. We came to a place where the river was much narrower and presumably safe to drive through. There were, however, dozens of cars parked, apparently unable to cross because the river was currently swollen. Our driver suggested that if we pushed from behind, the van could probably make it across the river. I didn't like the sound of things, but what else could we do? All of us (except Terrie) got out and pushed while the driver steered.

Halfway across the river, the van began to float and almost tipped over. Thankfully, the rear tires hit a large boulder. We caught up to it and kept pushing as the driver spun the wheels. Somehow—miraculously—we made it across and continued on to Matagalpa where we had a fruitful few days of ministry.

Looking back, it's an amazing memory. In the pressure-packed moments when we wondered if we would make it out alive, it was easy to question if we shouldn't turn around and go back. Even though we knew when we started that we might encounter some difficulties, we didn't expect them to be so dramatic. It was only by remembering why we were there and the reasons we were headed to Matagalpa that we were able to continue.

Something similar takes place on the journey of marriage. When a couple is first married, they know they have a journey ahead of them. And, at least in their minds, they know that there are sure to be a few bumps in the road along the way. But theoretical bumps in the road are different from experiencing real moments of conflict and seasons of frustration. It's like the difference between a mere pothole and being held up by guerrilla fighters. The first is uncomfortable; the second is disturbing.

Every marriage that lasts a significant amount of time, however, faces its ups and downs and seasons of difficulty. I remember about five years into our marriage when Terrie and I were alone in the car driving somewhere and got into a disagreement. I can't remember now where we were headed or what we were even talking about. But I do remember our frustration levels rising and Terrie finally saying, "Stop this car right now—I'm getting out." I did, and she did. We sat there on the side of the road—her outside and me inside—until we worked out whatever the problem was and could be in the same car together again. I'm thankful that through grace and forgiveness we were able to keep going forward.

It's not always disagreements that lead couples to these moments either. Sometimes it's just disappointment in general. Even though you told yourself that your expectations were realistic, somewhere in your heart you believed that marriage would be all bliss and romance. You forgot the realities of what it means to have two sinners in a close relationship that lasts for years.

It is during these times that we must pause to remember the big picture. We're not following a stranger in a motorcycle through the rainforest for the sheer adventure of it. We're not floating down a foreign river in a rented van for great scrapbook pictures. We have a larger purpose. For us in Nicaragua, the purpose was preaching and witnessing and encouraging pastors and churches. For you in marriage, there is a bigger picture than the moment as well.

In fact, there is a bigger picture than *you*.

In this chapter, we want to encourage you to step back and consider the ground we have covered in this book through a larger paradigm.

We told you at the beginning that we wanted you to have a greater goal for your marriage than that it would just be *okay*. We wanted to challenge you to cultivate an *awesome* marriage. In this chapter, we want you to look even wider. We want you to refocus from "Are we having an awesome journey?" to "What are the purposes of God for our marriage? Is our relationship bringing honor to Him?"

Ultimately, the purpose of marriage, as the purpose of every aspect of our lives, is to bring glory to God. Revelation 4:11 tells us that we are created for God's honor and pleasure: "Thou art worthy, O Lord, to receive glory and honour and power: for thou hast created all things, and for thy pleasure they are and were created." And 1 Corinthians 10:31 brings it a little closer to home as it instructs us to bring glory to God in every activity of our lives: "Whether therefore ye eat, or drink, or whatsoever ye do, do all to the glory of God."

Marriage has an added component of bringing God glory in that it pictures Christ's love for the church: "Husbands, love your wives, even as Christ also loved the church, and gave himself for it; That he might sanctify and cleanse it with the washing of water by the word, That he might present it to himself a glorious church, not having spot, or wrinkle, or any such thing; but that it should be holy and without blemish" (Ephesians 5:25–27). Thus, as Christians in the covenant relationship of marriage, we become representatives of the love Christ has for others. That is both a glorious and a sobering responsibility.

What does it look like in relation to the day-to-day aspects of marriage? How can we as Christian husbands and wives magnify Christ and, through our marriages, bring glory to Him?

UNDERSTAND THE PROCESS

As I mentioned a moment ago, a Christian marriage is a union of two sinners. When we trust Christ as our Saviour, we are born again and given a new nature (2 Corinthians 5:17). But our old habits and the temptations around us don't vanish. We still deal with the flesh, and that pulls us toward selfishness. God's plan for us is to conform us to the image of Christ—a process we call *sanctification.*

Sanctification lies between justification and glorification. Don't let all the *"ification"* words cause you to think this is complicated. It's very simple—and very important to understand.

Justification happens at salvation. It is when you are justified in the sight of God because the righteousness of Jesus is applied to your account. (See Romans 5:1.)

Glorification will take place when we receive our glorified bodies in Heaven. (See 1 Corinthians 15:42–44.)

Sanctification is the messy process in between as God conforms us to the image of Christ.

```
•————————————<<<<<>>>>>————————————•
Justification           Sanctification              Glorification
```

Romans 8:28–29 describes this process: "And we know that all things work together for good to them that love God, to them who are the called according to his purpose. For whom he did foreknow, he also did predestinate to be conformed to the image of his Son, that he might be the firstborn among many brethren."

Although we have already been justified before God, we have not yet been glorified in Heaven. Bible students sometimes say that "we live between the *already* and the *not yet*." This in-between place is the realm of sanctification.

When you keep the big picture in view, sanctification is an exciting process. To think that God wants to conform us into the image of Jesus is amazing. But in the day-to-day work of sanctification, it's not always so exciting.

And marriage adds a dynamic to this process because marriage has a way of exposing our *unsanctified* areas—

selfishness, insecurity, pride, and any other aspect of our lives not yet conformed to Christ—like no other realm of life. Marriage also has a way of giving us opportunities to die to self and cooperate with God's process of sanctification.

But when you forget that sanctification is in the middle of two awesome moments—justification and glorification—it's easy to become discouraged. Remembering the big picture and realizing that this land between the already and the not yet is full of opportunities to glorify God as you become like Jesus helps to keep it all in perspective. It motivates you to cooperate with God's purposes and to actively engage in what He is doing in your life.

Part of the adventure of sanctification for a married couple is remembering that the two of you are both on the same journey. So enjoy the journey, and give grace to one another as you come to swollen rivers and guerrilla fighters in the process.

SHARE AND SERVE ON THE JOURNEY

Conforming us to the image of Christ is not the only way that God is glorified in our marriages. He is also glorified as we bear fruit. Jesus told His disciples, "Herein is my Father glorified, that ye bear much fruit; so shall ye be my disciples" (John 15:8).

Part of this fruit, no doubt, is the fruit of the Spirit that comes as we yield to the Holy Spirit (Galatians 5:22–23), and that fits into the process of sanctification. But in the context of Jesus' conversation with His disciples, it would seem that His emphasis of fruit had to do with the fruit of souls trusting Christ. Just a few verses later, He continued, "Ye have not chosen me, but I have chosen you, and ordained you, that ye should go and bring forth fruit, and that your fruit should remain…" (John 15:16).

Don't miss this truth, because it has the potential to exponentially expand your understanding of the purpose of your marriage.

The word *ordained* simply means "set apart for a purpose." So God has chosen every Christian and set us apart for the purpose of bearing fruit. This happens as we share the truth of the gospel with others. Obviously, not all Christians are pastors or teachers, and not every Christian couple is called to what we think of as vocational ministry. But *all* of us are called to share the message of the gospel with those who don't know Christ. And *all* of us are called to serve others in Christ's name.

If you're not careful, it is easy to develop tunnel vision regarding your marriage. It is easy when you hit a season of difficulty to want it fixed simply to make your life more comfortable and your marriage more exciting.

But the purpose of our lives is not comfort; it is to bring glory to God. And the purpose of marriage is not excitement; it is that we would be able to serve God better together than we could individually.

God does not promise to make us comfortable, but He does call us to be conformed to His image. This is one of the reasons the local church is so important for a Christian marriage. In addition to the preaching and teaching ministries of a church, the church is to equip Christians toward spiritual maturity and the work of witnessing and serving. Ephesians 4:11–12 tells us that God gave "...pastors and teachers; For the perfecting of the saints, for the work of the ministry, for the edifying of the body of Christ."

If you are not actively engaged in serving through your church and regularly sharing the gospel with others as a couple, I would encourage you to find ways to make these activities regular parts of your life.

If you are a couple in ministry, I would encourage you to recognize the opportunities that witnessing and serving give toward strengthening your marriage and allowing you both to better fulfill its purpose of bringing glory to God. Sometimes couples in ministry get to a point where they begrudge the demands ministry makes on their marriage. Every occupation includes demands. (I would guess that surgeons and police officers face similarly unpredictable and demanding schedules.) Instead of resenting the burdens that come with ministry, look for ways to share the opportunities. Terrie and I enjoy serving together—inviting people to church, making visits, hosting members in our home, discipling couples, delivering loaves of homemade bread to widows, and praying for needs within our church family are all things we can do together. You cannot share in every aspect of ministry, but enjoy the ways you can share together as moments of spiritual and relational synergy.

Whether or not you are "in ministry," ask the Lord to help you catch a vision for your marriage that is larger than just the two of you and just your family. Ask Him to allow you to use the gift of marriage to synergistically make a difference for Him in the lives of others.

REFLECT GOD'S LOVE

Recently, Terrie and I had the opportunity to visit the country of Norway. Our guide on the Royal Palace tour was exceptional. She was clearly patriotic with a deep loyalty to the royal family.

She described the tumultuous turn of the century in Norway, which had been in intermittent union with other countries for over five hundred years. A king had reigned over Norway since AD 872, but for the previous five centuries, the king had been shared with other nations, most recently Denmark and Sweden, and had not resided in Norway.

As desire for independence from these unions grew, the Norwegian parliament reached out to a prospective king—Prince Carl of Denmark. Carl agreed to come, but only under the condition that the general population wanted a monarchial government in general and wanted him to be the king specifically. When word of this reached the Norwegian people, they wanted him more than ever, and the referendum confirmed this with an overwhelming 79 percent support. (Our guide even teared up as she relayed this portion of the story.) Prince Carl further endeared himself to Norway when he changed his name to Haakon, a name used by Norwegian kings five hundred years prior.

King Haakon VII arrived in November of 1905 with his wife and his young son Prince Olav. He would be the first king of Norway of the past several centuries to live in Norway. Upon his coronation, he assumed the motto, *"Alt for Norge,"* or "We give our all for Norway."

When the Nazi forces invaded Norway during World War II, the royal family realized they had two choices— exile or give the government up to the Nazis. They chose exile and led the parliament in choosing the same. From Great Britain where King Haakon and Prince Olav stayed, they used every means at their disposal to unite Norway in resistance toward the Nazi invasion and occupation. Haakon is remembered still for his significant role during this pivotal time in history. He lived to see the end of the war and Norway restored before he died in 1957, leaving the throne to his son Olav.

If King Haakon was revered, King Olav V was loved. In the 1930s, he served as a naval cadet and subsequently moved up the ranks of the military. During the war, he served in significant advisory capacities for the Allied forces, and once back in Norway, he led the Norwegian disarmament of the German occupying forces. So by the time he assumed the throne, Olav was already known and loved by his country.

Often referred to as "the people's king," Olav was extremely popular. He liked to drive his own cars rather than being chauffeured, and even took public transportation on occasion. When he once took the suburban railway on his way to go skiing, the press asked how he dared go out in public without bodyguards. "I have four million bodyguards," he responded. (The population of Norway was four million at that time.)

Olav served as king for thirty-three years. When he died on a cold January night in 1991, the people of Norway poured into the Palace Square. With hundreds of thousands of candles across the snow, the square was transformed into a sea of light, a bright tribute to a man who had given his all for Norway.

Our guide told us that these candles also served to assure Olav's son, Harald V, that the people of Norway still loved the royal family and wanted him to be their king. Almost with the pride of a grandparent showing pictures of her grandchildren, our tour guide showed us a picture of each member of the royal family and described how they were related, their place in the line of succession to the throne, and other details of their lives.

Norway is one of forty-three nations in the world with a monarchy, and we have had the privilege of visiting several of these—the United Kingdom, Liechtenstein, Luxembourg, Spain, and a few others. But never have we seen such loyalty and love for the royal family as we did in Norway, and particularly in our Norwegian tour guide. Our impression when visiting other monarchial countries has often been that many of the people tolerate the monarchy but would prefer another form of government. They may like some aspects of the history and the symbolism of the royal family, but in general, they would be just as glad to not have it.

But when our guide in Norway set down her pictures, she looked at us and, as if to explain the tears in her eyes, said, "We love our king."

You could sense that she reflected on and felt the benevolence and kindness of the monarchy. As Terrie and I stood there and listened, I couldn't help but think, *We should love Jesus the way she loves her king.*

When the world thinks of *marriage,* they often think of an empty, self-serving type of love. But God desires that Christian marriages would be a reflection of the love of Christ. If we will reflect on God's love for us, even as our Norwegian guide reflected on the benevolence of her king, we will become reflectors of His love to one another.

The apostle John wrote that the love of God for us should motivate us to give love to one another: "Herein is love, not that we loved God, but that he loved us, and sent his Son to be the propitiation for our sins. Beloved, if God so loved us, we ought also to love one another" (1 John 4:10–11).

God's plan for your marriage is that it would be a picture of Jesus' love for the church. But for this to happen, we must love God and love each other with His love.

GIVE YOUR ALL

King Harald V of Norway adopted the motto his grandfather first chose as king, *"Alt for Norge."* And, indeed, over the past century, that motto and the sacrifice behind it has proved to the people of Norway the love of their kings.

What do you think might happen in your marriage if you took the motto "We give our all for the other"? What do you think might happen through your marriage if you took the motto "Together, we give our all for God"?

Sometimes the needs in front of us seem overwhelming. How can we, as just two people, make a difference for the Lord through our marriage, especially in the midst of all the evil in our world? We look around us and feel discouraged. We look at ourselves and feel insignificant and insufficient. You may even look at your marriage itself and wonder how your singular efforts could make a difference against a relationship that seems unsalvageable.

You and I never know how God might use us or how He might miraculously work through us. And we never will know until we make ourselves fully available to Him. God never asks us to do more than we can do, but He does ask us to give our all for Him. "And whatsoever ye do, do it heartily, as to the Lord, and not unto men" (Colossians 3:23).

You can't halfheartedly invest in your marriage and expect full returns. And you can't halfheartedly invest together in the work of the Lord and expect miracles. Give your all.

When you do, you will find that God blesses our wholehearted efforts in ways we couldn't have even dreamed, and He gets the glory. "Now unto him that is able to do exceeding abundantly above all that we ask or think, according to the power that worketh in us, Unto him be glory…" (Ephesians 3:20–21).

SO…ARE WE THERE YET?

As we've seen in these pages, marriage is an incredible journey that is filled with many "Are we there yet?" moments. It's an awesome journey, but it includes unplanned, and often undesired, "adventures" along the way.

We live between the already and the not yet. And although the process of sanctification in between can be challenging and tiring and downright frustrating, it is full of opportunity to bring glory to God as we live for a purpose larger than ourselves.

So no, we're not there yet.

But yes, the journey we are on is awesome.

Don't give up in those moments when you don't think you can travel the journey even one more mile. There is a bigger picture than the setback you may be facing now. The road ahead holds new challenges, yes, but the challenges are en route to victories.

So, settle in, keep your seatbelts fastened, and decide this journey is going to make it all the way to the destination—together.

(top) Preaching in El Salvador
(left) Preparing for our river crossing
(right) Evening service in Nicaragua

With the Royal
Family at the
Palace in Norway!

THE LOVE OF GOD AND YOUR ETERNAL DESTiNATiON

It was my very first marriage counseling appointment. Terrie and I had recently completed Bible college and joined the pastoral staff of a dynamic church. With a fresh haircut, a suit, a Bible, a college degree, and a cubicle, I was eager to serve God in local church ministry.

An Indian couple, Hemat and Nanda, had called the church asking for marriage counseling, and I was eager to reach couples. So, despite the fact that I had never conducted any marriage counseling, I offered to meet with them in my spacious cubicle at the church office. I will never forget that appointment.

As we sat down, it was clear that Hemat and Nanda had tremendous tension and anger toward each other.

"How long have you been married?" I asked innocently.

"Ten years," he answered. You could sense the coldness in the air.

I pressed forward, "And what seems to be the problem that you are facing right now?"

"I hate him," she answered.

"And I hate her," he echoed.

"I see," I paused, a bit taken back. "And how long have you experienced these problems?"

"Ten years," they both said at once.

Wow. Ten years married and ten years of hatred. This was not what I was expecting.

As the story unfolded, I learned that Hemat and Nanda had an arranged marriage. Ten years prior, their fathers in India had met at a market, struck a deal, and bargained for their union. Not only had they never been in love, they never even liked each other.

With a bit of trepidation, I opened my Bible and began to share the gospel of Jesus Christ with Hemat and Nanda. They had a Hindu background and were used to thinking in terms of thousands of gods. What a joy it was to explain the One true and living God, and His gracious desire to save them and come into their lives.

They listened hesitantly, but as I shared the Word of God, I could see God working in their hearts. Their countenances softened, and their entire bodies began to relax. God was showing them that this was the truth which they needed for their lives.

Hemat and Nanda had many questions, and we met a few times before they bowed their heads and accepted Jesus Christ as their personal Saviour. That decision, however, changed their lives. And it changed their marriage as well as they now had the love of Christ in their hearts for one another and the power of God to help them build the relationship they had never developed.

Perhaps you have never heard or understood what I shared with Hemat and Nanda that day. Perhaps you are trying to make your marriage work without knowing Christ as your personal Saviour. Allow me to share with you what I had the privilege to share with them.

GOD LOVES YOU

We've said throughout this book that God designed marriage to be a picture of Christ's love for the church. The Bible tells us plainly that God loves the world, and He loves each of us.

In fact, the most well-known verse in the Bible emphasizes God's love: "For God so loved the world, that he gave his only begotten Son, that whosoever believeth in him should not perish, but have everlasting life" (John 3:16). He loves you. This is why Jesus came to earth.

WHY JESUS CAME

Jesus didn't come to earth some two thousand years ago just to encourage us or provide a good example. He— God in the flesh (1 Timothy 3:15)—came because we were separated from Him by sin.

We were all born with a sin nature that separates us from God. In Romans 5:12, we see that since Adam and Eve made the choice to disobey God in the Garden, a sin nature has been present in all people: "Wherefore, as by one man sin entered into the world, and death by sin; and so death passed upon all men, for that all have sinned."

Romans 3:23 tells us, "For all have sinned, and come short of the glory of God." Even the best of us are sinners.

Sin has a high price tag, too. Romans 6:23 says, "For the wages of sin is death...." In other words, the price for sin is eternal death, apart from God, in a lake of fire called Hell. Revelation 21:8 describes this place and those who go there: "But the fearful, and unbelieving, and the abominable, and murderers, and whoremongers, and sorcerers, and idolaters, and all liars, shall have their part in the lake which burneth with fire and brimstone: which is the second death."

Literally, this is where sinners (like you and me) are headed, apart from the miracle of Christ and what He provided for us.

YOU CAN'T EARN HiS LOVE

Many people—both religious and non religious alike—have misconceptions as to what we can do to make up for our sin.

Some believe that simply being "born into a Christian family" does the trick.

Others claim that if we do enough good works—give enough money, share enough kindness, love enough people, have a high enough standard of morality, or any number of "enough" whatevers—that this will at least make our good outweigh our bad.

Still others believe it has nothing to do with religion and that God judges only the sincerity of our hearts. They maintain that if we are sincere and consistent in our chosen belief system, He will overlook our faults.

God tells us, however, that eternal life is a gift. Romans 6:23 says, "…the gift of God is eternal life."

This is why Jesus came. Romans 5:8 explains, "But God commendeth [proved] his love toward us in that while we were yet sinners Christ died for us." The penalty for our sin is death, and Jesus Himself paid the price when He died for us.

Jesus Christ came to earth as God in the flesh, lived a perfect life, and then voluntarily died on a cross because He loves you. On that cross, He paid for all of your sins. He took your blame! What a gift—what love!

Three days later, Christ rose from the grave, and He now offers you this gift of eternal life and a personal relationship with God.

RECEiVE HiS LOVE

Although Jesus already paid for our sins and offers us salvation from sin and its penalty as a gift, we must choose to receive this gift.

Just as when you give your spouse an anniversary present, he or she has the choice to receive or reject that gift, so we have the choice to receive or reject Christ's gift of salvation.

To actually own the gift of eternal life, you must receive it; you must turn to Christ and place your full trust in Him alone as your personal Saviour. Romans 10:13 says, "For whosoever shall call upon the name of the Lord shall be saved."

This is a promise directly from God that if you will pray to Him, confess that you are a sinner, ask Him to forgive your sins, and turn to Him alone to be your Saviour, He promises to save you.

If you have never asked Jesus Christ to be your personal Saviour, you could do that right now. You could sincerely pray something like this:

Dear Lord, I know that I am separated from You because of sin. I confess that in my sin, I cannot save myself. Right now, I turn to You alone to be my Saviour. I ask You to save me from the penalty of my sin, and I trust You to provide eternal life to me.—Amen.

You'll never regret that decision. If you have just trusted Christ and received the gift of eternal life, we would love to hear from you. Please send an email to salvation@ strivingtogether.com. Additionally, you will find resources and Bible messages to help you grow in your relationship with God at our teaching website: dailyintheword.org.

NOTES

Chapter One

1. Matthew 19:5, Mark 10:7–8, 1 Corinthians 6:16, and Ephesians 5:31

2. If you have not been saved, you can be even right now. For a fuller explanation of what this means, please turn to the Appendix, p. 287.

Chapter Two

1. This is a book that I keep on hand and recommend often in marriage counseling.

Chapter Three

1. 1 Corinthians 7:3–5, Ephesians 5:22–33, Colossians 3:18–19, and 1 Peter 3:1–7

2. In his book, *Love and Respect: The Love She Most Desires, the Respect He Desperately Needs*, Dr. Emerson Eggerichs calls this "the crazy cycle." A husband is demanding to his wife, and she in turn cuts him down. She feels unloved, and he feels disrespected. Unless one of them will break the cycle, their responses will escalate in unloving, disrespectful ways. In reality, both spouses want the opposite of what they are refusing to give.

Chapter Four

1. Ashley Parker, "Karen Pence is the vice president's 'prayer warrior,' gut check and shield" (The Washington Post, March 28, 2017), https://www.washingtonpost.com/politics/karen-pence-is-the-vice-presidents-prayer-warrior-gut-check-and-shield/2017/03/28/3d7a26ce-0a01-11e7-8884-96e6a6713f4b_story.html?hpid=hp_hp-top-table-main_no-name:homepage/story&utm_term=.5eece2d36ab3

2. *The Choice Is Yours* (Striving Together Publications, 2011), 156–158.

Chapter Five

1. Some of the material in this chapter is adapted and expanded from chapter 12 of my earlier book *A Firm Foundation* (Striving Together Publications, 2004).

Chapter Six

1. The story of God's grace in the Walthers' life is an amazing testimony, and it is included in chapter 13 of my book *In Desert Places* (Striving Together Publications, 2011).

2. Jay Adams, *Christian Living in the Home* (P&R Publishing, 1972), 36–37.

3. I have lost track of where I originally discovered this resource, but looking these up recently, I discovered them at the website http://peacemaker.net/project/seven-as-of-confession/.

4. Corrie ten Boom, "Guideposts Classics: Corrie ten Boom on Forgiveness" (posted July 24, 2014, from a 1972 story in *Guideposts*), https://www.guideposts.org/better-living/positive-living/guideposts-classics-corrie-ten-boom-on-forgiveness

Chapter Seven

1. These are from *Marriage on the Rock* by Jimmy Evans (Inprov Ltd., August 2011, Kindle Locations 3915–3923), but I have added the Scripture references.
2. Jimmy Evans, *Marriage on the Rock* (Inprov Ltd., August 2011), Kindle Locations 3933–3939.
3. 1 Corinthians 7:3
4. Romans 14:23
5. A couple of books I sometimes recommend to men struggling with pornography are *The Purity Principle: God's Safeguards for Life's Dangerous Trails* by Randy Alcorn (Multnomah Books, 2003), *Finally Free: Fighting for Purity with the Power of Grace* by Heath Lambert (Zondervan, 2013), and *Addictions: A Banquet in the Grave* by Edward T. Welch (New Growth Press, 2012). While these are a good place to start, usually men need more than a book, including the help of a godly man who can provide counsel and accountability as you break free.
6. M.C. Black, et al., *The National Intimate Partner and Sexual Violence Survey (NISVS): 2010 Summary Report* (National Center for Injury Prevention and Control, Centers for Disease Control and Prevention, 2011).
7. Some of these thoughts are from the book *The Act of Marriage* by Tim and Beverly LaHaye (Zondervan, 1976), which was our primary text as a young couple learning to please one another in the acts of intimacy. While we have not gone in depth here, we do encourage married couples to read the LaHayes' book as a resource.

Chapter Eight

1. Amy Bernstein, "Dream On" (*U.S. News & World Report*, July 27, 1992).
2. For a short book on giving, see *Living on God's Economy: Ten Reasons to Place Your Financial Hope in the Promises of God* (Striving Together Publications, 2009).
3. Richard Swenson, *Contentment: The Secret to a Lasting Calm* (NavPress, 2013), 109.

Chapter Nine

1. Biblical scholars have speculated concerning the identity of Paul's thorn. Some believe Paul was referring to the continual persecution stirred up by unbelieving Jews throughout his ministry. Others believe he was speaking of an incurable eye disease that hindered his effectiveness. Galatians 4:13–15 seems to hint this direction. Whatever this thorn was, it was a constant and painful burden.

Chapter Ten

1. For more on the topic of scheduling and planning according to your life roles, see *Stewarding Life Planner* (Striving Together Publications, 2013).

Chapter Eleven

1. Fox News, "Photo of elderly man feeding wife on date night goes viral" (Foxnews.com, March 3, 2017), http://www.foxnews.com/health/2017/03/03/photo-elderly-man-feeding-wife-on-date-night-goes-viral.html

BiBLiOGRAPHY

Adams, Jay. *Christian Living in the Home*. P&R Publishing, 1972.

Alcorn, Randy. *The Purity Principle: God's Safeguards for Life's Dangerous Trails*. Multnomah Books, 2003.

Binney, Jim. *The Ministry of Marriage*. Faithful Life Publishers, 2015.

Chapman, Gary. *The 5 Love Languages: The Secret to Love That Lasts*. Zondervan, 1992.

Eggerichs, Dr. Emerson. *Love and Respect: The Love She Most Desires, The Respect He Desperately Needs*. Thomas Nelson, 2004.

Evans, Jimmy. *Marriage on the Rock: God's Design for Your Dream Marriage*. Inprov Ltd, 2011.

Harley, Willard F. Jr. *His Needs, Her Needs: Building an Affair-Proof Marriage*. Revell, 1986.

LaHaye, Tim and Beverly. *The Act of Marriage: The Beauty of Sexual Love*. Zondervan, 1976.

Lambert, Heath. *Finally Free: Fighting for Purity with the Power of Grace*. Zondervan, 2013.

Mack, Wayne A. *Strengthening Your Marriage*. P&R Publishing, 1977.

Rainey, Dennis and Barbara. *Starting Your Marriage Right: What You Need to Know and Do in the Early Years to Make it Last a Lifetime*. Thomas Nelson, 2000.

Scott, Stuart. *The Exemplary Husband: A Biblical Perspective*. Focus Publishing, 2002.

Swenson, Richard. *Contentment: The Secret to a Lasting Calm*. NavPress, 2014.

Thomas, Gary L. *Sacred Marriage: What If God Designed Marriage to Make Us Holy More Than to Make Us Happy?* HarperCollins Publishing, 2015.

Tripp, Paul David. *What Did You Expect? Redeeming the Realities of Marriage*. Crossway, 2010.

Welch, Edward T. *Addictions: A Banquet in the Grave*. New Growth Press, 2012.

ABOUT THE AUTHORS

PAUL AND TERRIE CHAPPELL live in Lancaster, California, where Dr. Chappell is the senior pastor of Lancaster Baptist Church and the president of West Coast Baptist College. His biblical vision has led the church to become one of the most dynamic Baptist churches in the nation. His preaching is heard on Daily in the Word, a daily radio broadcast heard across America. Terrie leads the ladies ministry of the church and hosts the annual West Coast Baptist Ladies Conference.

The Chappells have been married for thirty-six years, and they have four married children and nine grandchildren. Their children are all serving the Lord in full-time Christian ministry.

You can connect with Dr. Chappell through his blog, Twitter, and Facebook:

paulchappell.com
twitter.com/paulchappell
facebook.com/pastor.paul.chappell

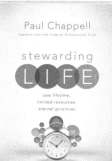
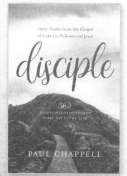

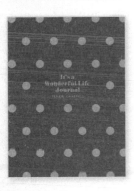
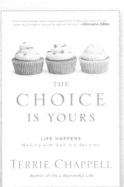

Visit us online

strivingtogether.com

wcbc.edu